Rough Cut Until I Bleed

Poetic Journeys, Volume 4

Charles Harvey

Published by Wes Writers and Publishers, 2020.

Rough Cut Until I Bleed

by

Charles Harvey

* * * * *

PUBLISHED BY:

Wes Writers and Publishers

Rough Cut Until I Bleed

While every precaution has been taken in the preparation of this book, the publisher assumes no responsibility for errors or omissions, or for damages resulting from the use of the information contained herein.

ROUGH CUT UNTIL I BLEED

First edition. March 24, 2020.

ISBN: 978-1878774156

Written by Charles Harvey.

Table of Contents

Rough Cut Until I Bleed (Poetic Journeys, #4) 1

69 5

The Duckbill Platypus at 3 AM 6

The Man in the Moon 7

Hunger 8

Fucking 9

I Know Why The Caged Bird Went Crazy 10

Youth is a Lie, and the Truth Ain't in It 11

A Disappearing Act 14

Rough Cut Until I Bleed 15

Windows 16

Boy Talk 17

A Boy and a Cigarette 21

Dealey Plaza 2015* 22

Summer Day 24

Miss Pearl's Chicago 27

Farting at Funerals and in The Museum of Lies 31

The Voyeur 33

Unfucked 35

Asses and Elephants..42

Grave Robber...44

Thirst 46

Young Men of the Cloth...47

I Am Not 49

A Dog and a Nightmare 50

The Journey Began at Fourteen....................................51

ANCESTRY.DOT.COM...53

Untitled...55

Dry Season 56

Adam 4 Adam..57

Make me wanna holla 59

Apocalypse 63

The Crazy Stories 66

THE WRAPPINGS HAVE BECOME UNGLUED 67

Bully..75

The THING 80

Happy..86

Charity 88

The Cicadas Have Landed 89

Mabel's Elephant Problem..101

About the Author 117

Epigram

Well, son, I'll tell you: Life for me ain't been no crystal stair. It's had tacks in it, And splinters, And boards torn up...

Langston Hughes

Table of Contents

69

The Duckbill Platypus at 3 AM

The Man in the Moon

Hunger

Fucking

I Know Why The Caged Bird Went Crazy

Youth is a Lie, and the Truth Ain't in It

A Disappearing Act

Rough Cut Until I Bleed

Windows

Boy Talk

A Boy and a Cigarette

Dealey Plaza 2015*

Summer Day

Miss Pearl's Chicago

Farting at Funerals and in The Museum of Lies

The Voyeur

Unfucked

Asses and Elephants

Grave Robber

Thirst

Young Men of the Cloth

I Am Not

A Dog and a Nightmare

The Journey Began at Fourteen

ANCESTRY.DOT.COM

Untitled

Dry Season

Adam 4 Adam

Poems from Selrach Devil

Make me wanna holla

Apocalypse

The Crazy Stories

THE WRAPPINGS HAVE BECOME UNGLUED

Bully

The THING

Happy

Charity

The Cicadas Have Landed

Mabel's Elephant Problem

About the Author

69

The world has secrets

behind Secrets and

puppets ruled by puppets.

You think the game is 69,

But you're a dog, Dawg

Chasing his rainbow tail.

Round and round you go,

Until you wake too late.

The catch is twenty-two

Three strikes and you're out.

The Duckbill Platypus at 3 AM

I'm lying awake thinking about the duckbill platypus.

Is it a duck or beaver? Is it a quack?

Does it love its parents June Cleaver and Donald Duck?

I heard June thought about scrambling it in a teaspoon of

Hot sauce to hide her infidelity. But luck said, "Let it be, let it be."

How does the duckbill eat? Who does it eat?

What's his politics? Does he talk out of both sides of

His Ping-Pong racket mouth?

What sport does he/she play?

I see a career in swimming or Frisbee. What's its kink in bed?

Hmmm with a mouth like that, I bet it's into spanking.

It's 3 AM.

Why is my dick all up in the duckbill's head instead of yours?

Why, baby? Why?

The Man in the Moon

Who's up at 2 am?

The midnight oil has long burned out

Sleep and sex roll restless

On the worn mattress.

Dreams escape open eyes

Shadows rattle the door

Three o'clock is the witching hour

Red ashes float from lips

Eyes across the courtyard catch you breathing

You look away only to look again.

You know your lonely mattress would enjoy the company

And your lilac-scented air could use some funk

But the night won't last a lifetime, so

You slip back into your room and wonder

What if there is a man in the moon?

Hunger

Walking through the house naked at 3 am

The air is your garment

Used Trojans cushion your feet.

You hear your roommate making love

With the one, you called *Dr. Spock*.

Your breath and dick brush the door

As you stand at the threshold and wonder,

If you should knock and ask to borrow

A cup of raw sugar? You don't need much,

Just a cup to dip your fingers in sweet stickiness,

Just enough to still your parched and trembling lips.

Fucking

It's 2 am

There ought to be

A poem between

Your legs.

I Know Why The Caged Bird Went Crazy

The thing we love is a prison,

Hands hold us like iron bars.

We bathe under watchful and lustful lenses

But hate those eyes and

Want freedom over yonder.

We have to love, because

We fear freedom,

Then hate the freedom we love,

Because, our wings fail under the sun's hot gaze.

We want to be in one another's dungeons,

Yet are grateful when we're not.

We love the stars and fireflies

Dancing outside our open windows

While we lockdown our hearts.

Youth is a Lie, and the Truth Ain't in It

Nights of dancing under stars

Making midnight twirl until

It rained men.

You slayed shirtless

Swam in foam and froth

Crawled over cum stuck floors

Go whores! Go Whores! Go Whores!

The fat DJ screamed and

Spun you around

Until drunk you fell down.

Fingers reached for any part

Of you they could prod and

Boy they needed to knead

Your ass and thighs.

You obliged and

Shot off to the moon

Just before the sun

Came into the office.

Eight days a night you roared

Vowing never to give it up.

Grace was God and Jones.

You sipped tea in rooms

In parks in the dark.

Clocks ran wild

Cocks swung wilder.

Sometimes you got clapped between the legs

And tiptoed through clinical doors.

Worried, you called your mama

Went to church until the devil

Declared you healed.

So now old men named

Byron, Nathan, Steve, Bob,

JoJo, Juan, Nick, Dominic—

Oh cute Dominic with dimples!

Who calls your name now?

Who envies your slow shuffle and big belly?

Who listens to your talk of yesterday?

Who cares how much coke you snorted and

Cocks you sucked in Mary's toilet, in the belly of

The Black Stallion, Jacks, or the Lavender Lounge?

"Who cares? Who cares? Who cares?"

Screech dead owls.

Your crew already in the grave

Patiently wait all day and all night

For you to bite the dust.

A Disappearing Act

The world,

It went away

Though blue as blue oceans

So blue it blinds the sun

And the moon winks

At the lacy clouds

Veiling her hair.

But when I look around

The world is gone

I reach out

To touch

And air fills my fingers

I reach out

To touch

And air fills my fingers

I reach out to touch

And nothing

Touches back.

Rough Cut Until I Bleed

Bleed I do

Bleed to death

Poems and poems.

The blood is not red

But blue black blue

Windows

I like open windows,

Their wide eyes

I like them high up,

Just high enough

From prying eyes

But low enough

For the right man

To catch the spirit

Of my open thighs.

I like showing my business

To sparrows, flies, and God.

Sometimes, when there is no man

I lie in front of the window anyway and wink

My brown eye at the chameleon

Turning all translucent on the glass

Except for his red heart beating itself to death.

Boy Talk

The First Time

It was sweet, sweet as a Popsicle

My first cock was, sweet and big

As a pickle in a five gallon jar

Sitting on a bodega counter

In Harlem.

It was juicy

Juicy as an orange in summer

It was full of blood and ill mannered,

Pushing my protesting tongue

Out of the way, the way

Big brothers elbow you

From the last biscuit.

It was wrapped in dollar bills

And smoke blazing towards

A dusty ceiling fan.

I wanted it because

That dimpled chin,

Soft plum-flavored lips,

And them dime colored eyes

Told me it would be something good.

It was.

################

Mine was black and sour

As old buttermilk

It pointed rudely to the right

Like a bat aiming at a skull

It was ugly and full of veins

I wanted to bite it

But the knife's blade

Glared in my eyes.

I obeyed the man

Who beat my Mother.

I endured his names

Of punk and faggot, uttered

Even as he choked me

On his cock.

I did it as he sat on the commode

His favorite seat in the house

His turds floated beneath my chin.

My life was no crystal stair.

I ran away at sixteen

He brought me back

And roped me to the

Chinaberry tree

behind the high fence.

He turned on his boom-box,

Grabbed three switches,

Made the air scream,

And dashed the remains of

His forty-ounce on my wounds.

He called for my mama

To bring him another

And another and another.

This dragon tattoo

Breathing fire down my back

Hides his malice,

But my wounds run deep

As I suck cock after cock

for bread and muscular arms.

A Boy and a Cigarette

Lips puckered like a sweet asshole

He takes a drag pulls it out

blows smoke rings in my face.

I inhale white circles, go back in

between his brass zipper.

I take the hog whole,

Grunt like an old boar.

I pull my lips away

The cigarette hangs

from lips puckered like a sweet asshole.

Ashes drift down and scorn me.

I go back in

The brass zipper has freed the hog

He roots for my tonsils,

forces a song from my throat,

swims in my vomit,

I call him Sir.

Dealey Plaza 2015*

Sirens wail like women

Motorcycles gun their throats.

A President's skull cracks open

Like an exploding egg.

Black cars speed by like panthers

Blood paints the sparrows red

Cardinals chant and moan

Leaves shimmer and shine.

A whale spits out Oswald

He has one deadly eye

Walks up to me

And points at the speck of him

In my dark pupils.

"I am innocent," he says.

A man named Ruby walks past

Holding thirty pieces of silver.

He tosses them into the air

Oswald calls tails

"Tails is death," Ruby says

"Last coin seals your fate."

The Kennedy Half Dollar blocks the sun

Bounces off a cloud, wobbles

Like it's wounded

Before landing face down.

Ruby pulls six triggers

Moves on, but takes a moment

To look at Oswald's ass

Bleeding blood and shit.

*Year I visited Kennedy Assassination Site

Summer Day

Summer rains come

Catch young men shirtless

Turn bodies to lacquer.

I taste their sweat

And am reminded of days

Loving madly in the rose garden,

Daring thorns to pierce my heart.

The Man at the Edge of Madness

It started with a pink cowboy hat

And a pink baton he used

To poke at women who turned

Their disinterested heads.

The black pants rose high

Over his ankles and shined

In the ass like dull glass.

The coat was blue corduroy

Even in the summer

Even in the rain.

Then the lights were disconnected

And he burned the land lady's cat

In the fireplace so he could write

And offered her the bones

But she was not having that

Nor his poems that went

Something like Plath

Itch itch itch itch

And the moon became his

Night companion on the nights

It felt like shining.

He threw a brick at a horses ass

But missed and dismounted a cop

In jail he lectured the iron bars

Until a deputy's fist knocked

His teeth all over the psych unit.

They let him go, pink hat and funky

Clothes. They kept the brick.

He wanders now and wonders

Why the stars are on fire.

He listens to the lamppost.

It tells him when he's hungry and

When it's time to shit, sometimes

Right then and there on Main in the middle

Of the lunch crowd who try to avoid his nature

And wonder what shit drove him crazy?

Miss Pearl's Chicago

The city goes to work on Monday

Grumpy and long faced it greets gray time clocks.

Giant yellow caterpillars dig into earth.

Clicking computers write Bullshit

In sixty-nine languages.

The city goes to work on Monday.

Chicago grooves on Tuesday.

Alert after two days of black coffee,

It makes conversation. Everyone

Has taped "Midgets Dancing With the Stars."

This diversion makes the city laugh sweetly and

Chicago grooves on Tuesday.

The city humps on Wednesday.

The computerized contracts

Sit like monuments on desks.

Fat Polish bosses sign them in blue ink.

The caterpillars chew out a hole large

Enough to bury two pyramids and a Sears Tower.

The grocery stores announce

"Hams—ten cents a pound"

'Cause cholera is killing

South American hogs and Strongmen.

The city shrugs its shoulders.

Thursday blows in from Lake Michigan.

State Street prisoners are anxious.

Got one more day to go,

One more contract to chew.

It rains at noon.

The city has busted a blood vessel.

There are hog guts all over the Loop.

Miss Pearl, head of Data Entry

Has just caught Chicago's third error.

She yells, *"There's a tub of*

Cow shit difference between 100

And 1000—Do you want the market to crash,

The world to end, to lose your job?"

"Hell yes," the City screams.

It goes home and beats its wife.

Blows echo like jack hammers.

Chicago is a perky as a young breeze on Friday.

The eagle has flown.

Miss Pearl gets a sweet kiss from

one of her blond "girls."

Wives recovering from Thursdays are

Invited to lunch. Blood roses

Match swollen cheeks. Promises are made

To buy "Beloved" a tiger coat.

On Friday Night, love is naked,

Bellies glide together.

The city makes its babies.

Chicago sleeps late on Saturday,

Yawns, fondles its privates,

Goes to breakfast at 11 a.m.,

Remembers ham is ten cents a pound,

Orders waffles, goes to the cleaners,

Retrieves the shiny night clothes of

Red satin and brass buttons.

Saturday night, State Street bathes in blood.

Liquor flows down hot bellies,

Miss Pearl's mouth earns her a toe tag,

Brains dissolve on sidewalks.

Rage rains in the city's heart.

Blood fills lonesome stockyards.

A barking dog causes a riot.

"Niggers" in Cicero incite Armageddon.

Skins are tender and heads thick,

Sirens wail and cry like mourners.

Chicago sleeps on Sunday

Gaped mouth and ugly,

Saliva dribbles on the clean white concrete.

Breath reeks fishy with dead semen.

The city buries Miss Pearl on top of old hog carcasses.

Chicago sleeps on Sunday.

Farting at Funerals and in The Museum of Lies

Do not fart in the African-American section

Of mask wearing spear-chuckers.

Do not fart there.

Go to the room of oiled portraits

Of buxom ladies, of cock sucking gents.

Go where the Madonna and child repose so peacefully

Upon downy clouds and, sapphire skies, and golden suns—

Go there to stink up the joint

With your day old collards, beans, onions, chitlins, and yams.

Fart until the room steams and empties itself

Of offended sensibilities.

Fart at grandma's funeral

As her pinched face swallows the formaldehyde

Offend Aunt Sarah and her Aunt too.

Offend! Offend! Offend!

What other weapons do you have, quiet one?

I am a good man, a decent man.

I go to church

And jack off to Jesus

Hanging on that cross

After being buggered by

By Roman cocks.

Lord, why have you left me?

Deacons have not been trained for my unholy dance

Museum guards have not studied quiet rebellions.

My voice is as muted as oils on canvases.

But here come the authorities, tongues caught in throats,

Imps come to deal with an odiferous devil

More rebellious than Malcolm, Mandela

Or Fidel could ever be.

The Voyeur

Stepping out of my skin

This old flabby suit—

I step into new skin and new life.

The camera records

Him scratching his balls

And sucking young cocks.

Most of us prefer

Two blue eyes but

For me one is enough

To observe his world.

And I do, like a guard

Watching the condemned.

He drives with piston power

All night long

Just pounding like a jack hammer

Asses yield with gratitude

Gaped, red, and juicy

As Texas grapefruit.

Lips slather his cock

With kisses and olive oil.

Legs part

One in the west and one in the east.

Suddenly I imagine I'm in new clothes

Blue Versace coat short enough

To give you a peek of my ass.

Even my new red drawers get in on the act

And cup my balls.

Arrayed in finery,

I turn on the camera

Grab my cock as just as he does.

We jerk, bust a nut together

Then slumber with our lips in separate rooms.

Unfucked

Maura reached to unlock her front door

Of wood and stained glass,

Of dreams and lips unrequited.

The door was ajar.

She turned and looked at Sidney's car parked in the drive.

I've told that man a million times to lock this door.

He left enough room for the devil and snakes to enter.

Maura shut the door with a soft click.

Sidney's briefcase sat where he normally parked it,

On the bottom step of the winding stairs.

My husband,

That—Everything has a place—man, Maura sighed.

She threw her purse on the couch and started to call Sidney's name,

But changed her mind. He was no doubt playing

Some silly game on the computer and wouldn't answer.

That's like a man—responding only to dinner and pussy.

Maura was thirsty.

Her drive home drained her of all liquid except blood

And the heat had parched her lips.

She slipped into her kitchen.

Two glasses sat on the counter—

One half full one half empty.

That was Sidney's favorite riddle.

And he was a man of riddles.

He could love her all day with words

And birdlike pecks on the cheek

But leave her unfucked at night.

As fresh water splashed into her clean glass,

Maura thought she heard a moan.

The devil, Maura said to herself and cocked her head.

(Unfucked continued)

Silence.

"What's there to say in the house of an unfucked woman?

What are these walls whispering about?

Nothing at all." She sighed and continued filling her glass.

As she drank, a voice cried out,

"Fuck me into jelly, baby!"

"Surely that's the devil, but what does he want with me?

Jezebel doesn't live in this tomb of chrome and glass,

Of pecks on the cheek and a twat untouched.

What does the devil want with me?"

Maura stood at the stairs leading to her bedroom,

Pondering over Lucifer, who by now

Had groaned four times like a man in the gas chamber.

She looked at her watch. It was only four in the afternoon.

Perhaps she should have warned Sidney she was coming home early.

For all she knew

He might be in bed with a bottle of champagne

And her panties atop his head like a crown

Entertaining some whore.

She had seen that act in a magazine.

But that woman got fucked. Even the champagne bottle

Had gotten into the act.

"How is it that a bottle can be more fun than a man?"

Maura wondered then. Now as a married woman she knew.

She tipped up the stairs,

Got halfway until *"Bitch*!" stopped her.

She looked over her shoulder,

"Surely the devil is in these walls mocking me."

A hand slapped against flesh. More sighs and moans

Tumbled down the stairs to where she stood

The voice was unfamiliar—deeper than Sidney's.

The tongue might have been attached to a ghetto street corner

To a man picking up his ego from the sidewalk

After being scorned by a woman.

Maura wondered if she was dreaming, and should she hike her dress—

Hike it to the sky and let the garment fly her away like a kite.

By now she was at the top of the stairs.

Standing by the *Montage of Bees Buzzing Through Sunflowers.*

This was Sidney's favorite painting. Splashes of yellow and black burst

Through the white walls and made her dizzy.

(Unfucked continued)

Their bedroom door peeped open

Like an eye disdaining the morning light.

Maybe he was watching porn and jerking off, Maura thought.

Jack-off in the toilet, rinse, and repeat,

Leave the wife unfucked.

She started to let Sidney have his moment.

But thought about the two glasses on the counter—

One half full, one half empty.

Maura stood at the doorway to her bedroom.

Moans and sighs sang in her ears. Her breathing slowed.

She wondered why that bitch's twat was getting fucked

While hers lay discarded like a dead fish in the mud.

The tall *African Fertility Sculpture*, with jutting breasts and moon face,

Beckoned from a stone pedestal.

"*Make me your sword, so that I may smite that whore.*"

Maura paid no attention.

After all, despite his contradictions,

Sidney filled up the space around her,

Opened tight jars and carried the heavier bags of groceries.

He liked her spaghetti and called her "*honey.*"

They did a little sex thing every other Friday.

He was enough husband.

Fertility laughed and shook her head.

"*Enough husband,*" she mocked Maura.

Maura tossed all reasoning aside,

Snatched *Fertility* off her pedestal,

And pushed open the door

The first thing she saw was Sidney's feet high in the air,

As if he was flying on a playground swing.

She noticed how clean and pink his soles looked—like child's feet.

She looked past the foot, ankle,

Down his tan leg, and past his knee shaped like a red potato.

Her eyes suddenly shifted to the mirror hanging above the dresser.

She couldn't look directly at the ass gyrating between her husband's knees.

It seemed rude to stare at the winking eye

In the middle of the Devil's black ass.

Below the buttocks hung the Devil's horse balls,

Slapping and swatting Sidney's ass.

Swack, swack, swack.

While Maura stood unfucked

Holding onto *Fertility*.

Asses and Elephants

They shit from their mouths

Diamond laced turds and

They piss gravy platitudes

Blah blah blah

And the sheeple go

Baa baaa baaa

As soundbites of bullets

Fly over their heads:

Lower your taxes

Order your laws

Save your jobs

From Mexican mobs

Watch me make love to your

Stars and bars

Bend over so I can

Make America great again

Blah blah blah

Secrets behind secrets

Puppets stringing puppets

The people the people

Throats and eyes caked

With bullshit

Go blindly into nuclear night.

Grave Robber

That boy did not look like

His beautiful living self. Did not.

That undertaker must be blind.

That boy did not look like himself.

His other self was black and sensuous

Like a sable coat draped over David*

That undertaker left all the black, but

Blew the beauty up his nose.

That boy had been a peacock

That undertaker turned him into a crow.

Mourners look up from the grave

And screech like monkeys

Lo and behold

The undertaker is wearing that boy's face

Sewed over his own wrinkled mug.

Left a diamond brooch stuck

In that boy's chest.

As if jewels are more beautiful than beauty.

*Michelangelo's David

Thirst

I need a poem

But none will come

So I cover the page

With **********

***************'s

for all the words

that should have been.

Young Men of the Cloth

We goin to

Fuck it up muck it up

Truck it up suck it up

Dick it up.

We goin to jazz June

Make summer bloom

Die soon.

Then we goin to rise

Take up our cross

And floss

Make us a religion

Invite you to worship

Us gods

All night long

Until the purple

Peeks through

The moon of your chariot

Waiting

To bear your tired bones

On up to heaven.

I Am Not

I am not a not

Even if I have no home

And have to roam

From box to bridge

And sleep skull to

Sidewalk. I am not a not.

A Dog and a Nightmare

Who is this that comes in the dark

Who presses against the small of my back

And my shoulders? I want to kiss him

But instead I curse and shout the twenty-third psalm,

"The Lord is my shepherd."

Sometimes he leaves right away

And sometimes he lingers longer

Turned on by my struggle.

He digs his fingers into my ass.

I look forward to his coming

Not the lord's but this thing

I look forward to his pressing, and pressing me

Into the bed.

When he's had enough of me

I hear bedroom door go thump

And my ass twitches a little.

"A man is a dog and a nightmare," my mother said

I agree, a dog and a nightmare.

The Journey Began at Fourteen

Men been looking at me

Since I was fourteen

Been looking and looking and looking—

Old black men, young niggas,

When I look back, they look off

When I look back, they look off

When I look back, sometimes

They look back, hands go to crotch, heads nod.

My blood rises and settles in my dick.

At fourteen, I didn't know why.

I tried to ask Jesus once

But my eyes couldn't go past

His burnished thighs

And that skimpy loin cloth.

At seventeen, my answer came in a troubling dream

My father lay across my back

And his hot fingers probed my ass hole.

After that

On late night walks

Car doors opened for me

Dark corners lit by eyes and headlights became my home

There I roamed.

"Sup, man?" was the riddle.

My silent lips answered.

Back seats groaned and

My feet danced in rear windows.

Sweet sweat covered our bodies.

I preferred memories over money.

Dollars go up in smoke

But journeys last a lifetime.

ANCESTRY.DOT.COM

Which bodily fluid

Says the most about

Where your bones

Come from?

Dot.Spit? Dot.Shit?

Dot. Dot. Dot,

I asked the electronic test tube

Am I Masai warrior

Cousin to Shaka Zulu?

Or do I hale from the great

Pigmy shorty shorts?

Is this Watusi in me

More than a dance from the 60's?

Do the watusi, do the Hutu!

Do in the Tsuisi

That boy got rhythm in his blood

"Not so fast," says dot.com.

You got white blood in you too

Courtesy of Nigeria in 1689

In the name of the King of England.

Dot.Jism say Hoi who cut your hair

In Asian barbershop your cousin

Not Barbara Brown or Charlie Brown

Dot. Dot. Dot

Dot.Come. Dot.cum. Dot.jism///

Send in your cash

Com. Com Com

Your bones yearn

To know truths and proofs

Your bones are lonely

Need to know their place

In the vast vat of universe.

No man is a mountain by himself.

Untitled

The boy plies his trade

In weeded lots just beyond

The starry-eyed metroplex.

He is in college, cold, and poor

If he misses his meal ticket

It's sardines for lunch.

White men crave to lynch him, crave to love him

Crave to own him, crave to mourn him.

Emotions swing like switchblades and ropes.

He knows he's sweet poison.

On his back peering through

Half moon roof while getting his dick sucked,

He contemplates the day he will

Earn his bread behind a glittering desk.

He won't prostitute no more

He'll be a badass bidness man, legit,

Will have a license

To sell his ass to the highest bidder.

Dry Season

"It's been a long dry season,"

Said the page.

"My skin is withered and brittle."

"Lord, yes," said the pen.

"My blood has clotted

And my body has lost its spring.

Oh look! His old hand approaches."

"Rest yourselves young ladies,"

Spoke the hand. "He ain't messing

With y'all today.

He's curled me into a spasm

Trying to stroke some life

Out of that old ding-a-ling

He carries between his legs.

It's been a long dry season."

Adam 4 Adam

Arms and legs

Torsos galore

Dicks, asses

a foot or two

But no eyes

To peer into

The soul with.

No mouth

Telling me

"I love you."

And no ear shells

I can whisper back into

I love you

I love you

I love you

Poems from Selrach Devil

Make me wanna holla

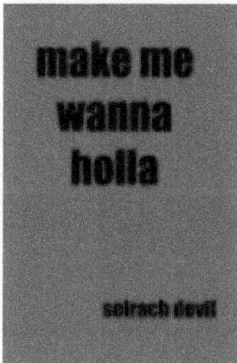

A moose rode the caboose

While smoking a deuce.

What you say?

I say a moose rode the caboose

While smoking a deuce

What he do that for?

He a moose

And he smoked?

A deuce

And he rode?

A caboose

And his story?

A moose rode the caboose

While smoking a deuce

Okay...and his mama?

She gone walking Fifth Avenue selling pussy

And his papa?

Gone mad on fry

And his God?

Thrown the book at him

And his teacher?

Dreaming of girl tits

And his preacher?

Trying to get his dick

And his God?

Thrown the book at him

And himself?

Riding the caboose

And the train?

Derailed in Detroit

Preempted in Harlem

Gun shotted in Chicago

Gangbanged in LA

And himself?

Don't know what to do

And his money?

Be funny

And his President?

Be black and don't matter

And his congress?

Assuming he the problem… pointing all five fingers at him.

And him need?

Heaven

And his Heaven?

Closed for budget cuts

And his angels?

Fucked up

And his moose?

Riding that caboose 'til the cows come home

And them cows?

Getting fat in Afghanistan

And his war?

Cut off his arms, his leg, almost his nuts

And his Marvin Gay say?

Make me wanna holla the way they do my life.

Apocalypse

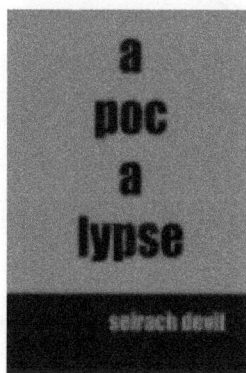

I don't give a fuck

About Donald Duck

Cluck! Cluck! Cluck!

He a chicken shit

He a mouth too small to

Blow smoke up my ass

But he sure blowing jazz

Up some white folk's corn holes.

He blowing smoke, and they

Inhaling the shit he shit.

He gonna paint the White House red

From the blood of busted skulls,

'Cause the cops are coming

The Neo-Nazis are coming

The skinheads are coming

The KKKs are coming

The Jew haters are coming

The nigger haters are coming

The stars and bars are coming

The Uncle Toms are bowing,

"Yas suh! Yas suh!" thirty pieces of silver

to seal they thick lips.

They raising Bull Connor from the dead

The fools have been fooled

The turkeys are coming home to defecate,

But the wise will rise

From the ashes of democracy.

The Crazy Stories

This book wouldn't be complete without some dystopian craziness. These stories might reflect the future of the USA. What comes after Donald Duck has killed democracy and sent US following the path of dinosaurs. BTW there's more than four stories. So grab your glasses again.

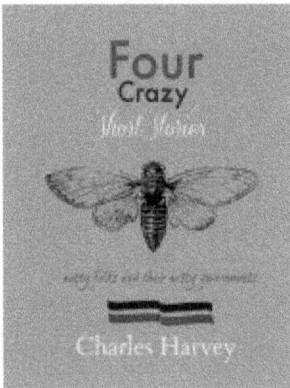

THE WRAPPINGS HAVE BECOME UNGLUED

Thomas Jefferson Roosevelt carefully smoothed the rough brown paper. He neatly tucked in the excess bits and edges. He made sure the tape was straight and even. Each piece that crossed the other had to do so at perfect ninety-degree angles. When he was through, the package was as smooth as polished marble. He sat it on the table and looked at it. He smiled and rubbed his hand over its surface. He had labored over the package for thirty-six hours, using two rolls of brown paper, two spools of clear sticky tape, and three balls of string. All of this for a ten-by-ten cube.

At times, a wrinkle in the corner of the package had so angered Roosevelt, he ripped the paper off and started over again. When he looked, the line had moved to the cube's other corner. He spent hours fighting air bubbles that got under the paper and made the package look puffy. For a countless number of times, the tape had refused to line up correctly as Roosevelt brought it around the box's circumference. It was always unaligned by a fraction of a hair. Once when he thought he had it all polished off, Roosevelt found the item which should have been inside, was outside the package. He seriously thought of mailing the empty box rather than disturb the wrappings. But he went through the wrapping ritual again.

That was all behind him now. Every letter on the parcel was an even half-inch in height and one-eighth inch apart. Three-quarters of an inch separated each word. The Senator's name was spelled correctly: PETER ZBREGHANOFF.

Somehow Roosevelt spelled the last name quickly. Each letter from Z to F flowed from his felt-tipped pen like liquid black velvet. But that confounded Peter—was it Petre or Peeter? Maybe it was Pter, he thought. He had had to scan his Bible starting from Genesis through Deuteronomy, Job, and the Psalms until he got to the New Testament to find the correct spelling.

Now the clock with the pig's face was on its way to the Senator. The Senator had never answered any of Roosevelt's letters. Typical of the letters was this one:

Your Grace Senator Pter Zbreghanoff:

It is my duty to inform you of these matters concerning foreign policy. I personally met with the Russian Ambassador yesterday. We had lemonade. We decided during our caucus that the state of affairs in the world were incongruent with God's plan of salvation in our lives. We decided to work diligently to correctify this situation.

With sincere sincerity,

The Honorable Thomas Jefferson Roosevelt

P.S. The dogs bark too loud at night. The mayor refuses to answer my letters or calls. Can you help me?

"Perhaps the Senator never had time to write me, but this beautiful clock will change all of that," thought Thomas Jefferson. "It is a technological marvel too. The Senator will like that. He is always inspecting rockets, missiles, and guns. Fat devil."

To wind the clock, the pig's tail had to be twisted clockwise. To set the time, its nose had to be turned counterclockwise. To shut off the alarm, one had to just flick the pig's ear.

Roosevelt put the leftovers of his labors into a black leather satchel. The satchel resembled an old elephant's hide. It contained his tattered folder of yellowed resumes and a bundle of dusty letters stating:

"Unfortunately your qualifications do not match the position." He looked at the packets, frowned, and quickly shut the satchel.

Roosevelt eyed his package. Looking at it made him smile again. He imagined the Senator sitting in a walnut colored room writing a great speech. The speech contained such high phrases as "Peace through plutonium," and "Truth will burn through clouds of atomic dust." An Aide in white gloves bore the cube majestically on a silver tray toward the Senator's large nose and curious eyebrows, Of course, a smart young soldier in a green uniform had dropped the package off at the Senator's mansion. It got into the soldier's hands through a high Post Office official. Suddenly Roosevelt froze in mid-thought.

"Those fools at the Post Office!" he shouted aloud. "1 have gone down there, begging them on my knees pleading with then not to throw my packages around."

Roosevelt remembered the incident with a clerk who—with fat fingers weighted with red and blue jewels—listened attentively to his plaintive pleadings and remonstrations. When he had finished, he gave her a package containing a cat's head tenderly as if he was a Mother handing a new-born baby to a saint. She viciously stamped big purple marks all over it and flipped it backward without looking, into a cart of dirty, mangled boxes. She flashed her big yellow teeth and told him to have a nice day.

"What can I do to prevent this great package destined for the monumental Senator from suffering the same fate?" Roosevelt asked himself. He sat and thought for many hours. "I could ask to be sent with the package. I could attach razor blades to it, but that would mar its beautiful surface. I could send it by long white limousine. It will do no good to write the words 'delicate crystal' on it. No good at all!" Roosevelt had once written those words on a package of letters containing excerpts from meetings of Chinese Scientists he said he claimed he had met. He enclosed each letter in an empty baby food jar before placing them in a box. A tall bushy haired man at the Post Office played basketball with the package. He stood in a squat position with the parcel balanced in the palm of his hand. He bounded up on tiptoes, flipped his wrist downward, and slammed the package into an iron cart.

Roosevelt sat ruminating over these past events when an idea hit him so hard, he jumped up and kissed himself in the broken mirror on the wall. "I will simply write on the package, CAREFUL BOMB INSIDE. He wondered why he hadn't thought of that sooner. He had seen it on television hundreds of times. Men tiptoed through darkened corridors carrying tubes bundled in black tape as if they were handling sacred scrolls. They always put the package into the back of a thickly padded truck and drove it with the greatest of ease away from a building.

Roosevelt wrote the words carefully in thick black letters. The paper and pen squeaked in unison with each stroke of his pen as if they agreed with his idea.

"Now this will awake those klutzes. They will handle this clock as if it's a Faberge' Egg. It'll ride atop of other packages with imperious majesty. There'll be no bouncing this bundle around," said Roosevelt to himself. When he was finished, he put on his floppy knitted cap and adjusted it by turning it at various angles upon his head. After many hours in the mirror, he settled on a Parisian model affectation marked by the cap's bill slanting over his left eye. If only he had a cigarette and pouty lips, he thought. He checked for wrinkles in his short bellbottom tweed pants and, smoothed his red faded satin shirt. A thick, tattered wool overcoat completed his ensemble.

"Where is your staff, Your Majesty," Roosevelt asked himself, bowing low in the mirror. "Thank you, Lord Chamberlain," Roosevelt answered. He reached for the package and a broomstick handle with a feather duster tied to it. He quietly shut the door behind him. A black, bony dog got up on his unsteady legs and wagged his keen tail at Roosevelt. "Mr. President," said Roosevelt slightly tipping his cap. With the dog lurching behind him, Thomas Jefferson Roosevelt began his trip.

The walk was interrupted at times when Roosevelt stopped and commanded the dog, "Precede the King, you fool!" *Mr. President* flopped down on his swollen belly, opened his black mouth, and let out a long whining yawn. When Roosevelt turned and marched forward, the dog got up and limped after him. Two girls with stiff dark ponytails skipped rope in his path. They stopped and held their noses as Roosevelt approached. One girl giggled and pointed at his open fly. He aimed his broomstick at them as if it were a spear and grunted. They ran away screaming for their mothers.

"When will they learn to respect their King, the ruler of Zimbabwe and all its capitals?" Roosevelt shouted. He carried his head high and walked along, stopping every six steps to pound his staff to the ground. A woman saw him and went immediately to the other side of the street.

"That's more like it," he said as he saluted her with a wave of his hand.

"Hey, Do Funny!" Two old women sitting on a rickety porch, drinking sugar water called to him. He stopped and made the sign of the cross at the women and shook his rear end at them.

"Lord, have mercy. What kind of Priest is that," one snaggle-toothed woman asked laughing.

"That's your boyfriend," her pal teased.

Their cackling altered his gait and he lurched forward slightly stooped. He vaguely remembered himself a week ago wrapped in heavy red velvet curtains a funeral home had thrown out.

"Fool I was no priest. I was on my way to my coronation," Roosevelt said to himself. The old women's "stupidity" disturbed him, and he felt annoyed until he turned the corner and saw the red, white and blue flag hanging limply on a pole in front of a squat beige building.

"Stonehenge!" Roosevelt shouted and waved his staff at the building.

****

"Sir, you must wear shoes in the Post Office to be served," said a skinny blonde woman with buckteeth.

"I walk on the robes of Jesus, and my feet are comforted," said Roosevelt as he made the sign of the cross with his left hand. He knelt and kissed the cold, dirty floor. The clerk rolled her eyes and said nothing else. Thomas bowed at the assortment of people in line. A young woman with long brown hair smiled briefly at him. He grinned and sought her blue eyes. She turned and pretended to be interested in the framed list of former postmasters on the wall. Overwhelmed by his stench, she pulled her collar up to her nose. He greeted her warmly.

"I say your head is still pretty upon your shoulders Lady Anne Boleyn, but beware of Henry."

She screeched and darted out the door, leaving Roosevelt next in line. In the background, clerks shuffled about. They sailed little envelopes and postcards into honeycombs and cubbyholes. They smacked gum. One walked, juggling four or five parcels in the air. Roosevelt looked at the warning on his package and grinned. He waved to the man. A woman, the color of dark brown sugar sat in front of an enormous orange machine. She smiled and cooed into a telephone, pursing her lips as if she was blowing bubbles into the receiver. Her eyes were far away from her task. A procession of letters marched in front of her stopping a millisecond for a beam of light. At intervals, she touched a button and a letter was expelled into a basket beside the machine. They lay in a pile like unwanted fish

"Next!" the puffy faced clerk barked. Her brown hair was piled high on her head like coils of hemp. Her ample bosom heaved and rose like a battleship riding the waves. The soft black fuzz around her lips held little glass beads of perspiration. Gold chains cut into her thick neck. Her stubby fingers were ringed with gold, diamonds, and clear green stones. "Next!" She barked again. Her face turned red.

"Imagine, a mere clerk, a subject of the King, having more jewels than his Majesty himself," snorted Roosevelt.

"What did you say?"

"Nothing, Madam. I am simply a messenger boy of the Lord sent to deliver this package to the honorable Senator." Roosevelt bowed to her. The clerk snatched the package and slammed it hard on the iron scales.

"How do you want it to go, Parcel Post or First Class?"

"Why Madam, born on the backs of angels of course."

The clerk stared at him. A stray hair fell and tickled the side of her face. She jammed it under a hairpin. She narrowed her eyes at Thomas Jefferson Roosevelt. A glob of fatty skin pushed from the side of her neck. Roosevelt remembered he hadn't eaten a thing all day.

"Whatever is best. Just be gentle is all I ask," he said softly

She raised her thick arm to stamp a purple mark on the parcel. Roosevelt saw the word BOMB reflected in her huge square eyeglasses. Her pupils grew wide. She stared at Roosevelt, who stood smiling. She put her ear to the package and heard its faint ticking. Her face flushed white as milk. She pressed a button underneath the counter, and a loud honking like that of a goose was heard throughout the building. The slow clerks dropped their bundles and headed for the nearest doorway.

"He's the one who brought that package!" shouted the woman to the armed men in green who came running as she pushed her thick rear through a little passageway. Roosevelt smiled.

"My armed sergeants come to greet their king! Be men. Do not approach me like ballet dancers in pink underpants! Come forward. Now you can put me down. For God's sake, put down your sovereign! Put me down, but not in this mud you idiot! This rough treatment will most certainly earn the Senator a telephone call from me. Fool, get your boot off Mister President's tail! How dare you, cretin, dunk the Senator's elegant clock in that pool of muddy water. You've obscured the face! How will he know the truth now?"

In the wake of the commotion Roosevelt caused, dust and bits of envelopes floated and settled on the tables and chairs. The clerks, in a hurry to escape the bomb threat, had stomped and torn letters and packages with their heavy boots. The woman in front of the orange machine had left it running and it had ground some parcels in its toothy gears. In the midst of this wreckage, a brown package lay on the floor busted open and spilling its guts of green cabbage leaves imprinted with, the faces of President Hamilton and Statesman Franklin. This package also was addressed to Senator Peter Zbreghanoff.

###

Bully

I looked up and saw reflected in a distant mirror, this hefty soft-faced man between two old crippled women walking away from me. When they got to the corner of the glass wall, my man and his two ladies suddenly disappeared. It was as if a huge mirrored blade had chopped them from my vision. I shifted my eyes to the left and there they were again, coming toward me, gaining height with each slow step they took.

Seems like I had been sitting all morning in my yellow laminated chair in Sears' gray-walled waiting room, getting ripped off by the minute. My mama's little car was in their big shop. All I could do before my Savior and his Mary and Martha appeared to me in this vision was sit and watch the clock on the wall. Except it wasn't a real clock like nine o'clock, ten o'clock, et cetera, et cetera. It was a Sears dollar sign clock ticking off the dollars they were making off women and weak men like me. At first it started off slow because there weren't too many customers there in the early morning. So it inched: One dollar . . . One dollar . . . One dollar . . . One dollar . . . Its speed quickened as an odd lot of souls filled up the waiting room. It ran so fast, I couldn't keep up with it. Like a jazz man's horn:

one one one one one . . . dollar!

one one one one one . . . dollar!

one one one one one . . . dollar!

one one one one one . . . dollar!

That noise beat on my ears. A mad saxophone player filled the room with his insanity. My eyes got all crossed trying to keep up with the digital readout running across the clock's face like a flow of red water. I couldn't stand it anymore. That's when I noticed them.

My hefty man had on a pure purple lace shirt, brown flannel-like pants that flapped around his ankles, and his brown and white wingtips were ready to spread their wings and fly! He wore a vest and cowboy hat too. He walked right between those two crippled women. The three of them plodded like old mules. One old lady was blue-black. She had on a white t-shirt with Mickey Mouse on the front (her jutting bosom made Mickey's ears elephantine), red stretch pants that stretched from Houston to Odessa. She leaned on a four-pronged walker and lumbered like an old hippo. The other ancient puss was the color of my beautiful orange/brown man. And bless her poor lame self, when she sat down her lime dress flew up, and her thighs went their separate ways. Her chintzy black wig was an unruly swatch of poodle hair, shining and fully blessed by the fluorescent lights. Old Brown Boy sits next to me. His rump hit the seat and stirred up a funny smelling breeze that sneaked into my nose and down my throat.

"Man, I got me some trouble this morning. I got hands full of trouble," he said half smiling and squinting his gray trout eyes at me all at the same time. Then his trouble started yapping at him.

"Bully! I say, Bully! You gone let your mama and your Aunty die of thirst in this here steaming room? Get up off your behind, boy, and get us a Coke!" Her wig bounced up and down and all them gray hairs underneath peeped out and waved at everybody. Bully got up like a man who carried his trouble in his rear end.

"I don't want no coke. Ain't they got orange Nehi?" Bully's Aunt asked.

"Lord, Gladys, I ain't seen a Nehi sodawater in years. Let Bully buy you a Coke or a Seven—up.

"I want a cup of coffee!"

"Aunt Gladys, there ain't no coffee here," Bully half whined.

"There's coffee somewhere in Houston!"

"Gladys, I swear, you sure is contrary," said Bully's mother.

"Aw go on and get me a Coke. Shoot!"

Bully grasped both sides of the red and white vending machine and leaned forward. He studied the selection buttons like a man reading names on a memorial. Bully dropped his coins into the slot, letting each one trip the machine's registers and make that electronic gargling sound before dropping the other. The cokes crashed down the chute like clattering bowling pins.

"Oh Bully! Do you have to make so much noise! If you didn't want to buy the things why didn't you say so?"

"Mama, what you want me to do, reach my hand up in there and pull them out? That's a machine. I ain't got no kind of control over it."

"Inez, I told you a long time ago you ought to have put a strap across his naked ass when he was growing up. Look how he talks to you now.

"Hush up, Gladys. Just because you beat your child to a cripple..."

"She deserved every lick. Bully, this thing ain't cold!"

"Mine ain't either," Bully's Mama said. "Neither is my heart."

"I doubt if you'll be invited to sit at any Saint's table soon," Bully's aunt retorted.

Bully sat down next to me again. His knee brushed mine because I was sitting wide-legged and mannish. I moved my leg away a little and again his knee sought mine. I got mad. I wondered why this lace cowboy was trying to invade my space.

"Man, I got me a lot of trouble. You want some of my trouble?" He squeezed my arm with his soft hand and smiled. "Just look at them. Ain't they beautiful?"

I looked at the old women slurping their Cokes, their fish lips trembling, their legs gapped; Aunt Gladys' wig sitting cockeyed, and Inez's stretch pants about to explode. They were Halloween and Mardi Gras sitting side by side. I looked at Bully. There was a thin mustache above boyish lips—thin and petulant, slightly upturned. Lips that I kissed when I was nineteen. Carl Anthony! Lord. Lord.

God, you let the devil cut his body to ribbons in that filthy bookstore. Men too busy to notice him dying groped each other and danced in that boy's blood. I don't want to go back to those memories. Tell your imp to slay this memory. I don't want to grieve all over again. Grief is my constant lover. Grief led the chorus at my Father's funeral.

"Who killed Bully Red with that sweet sweet potato pie?" Fingers pointed at my Mama and Aunt Gladys. My Father had sowed his seed in both women and was going to leave them for another woman. Grief, secrets, and hate joined us.

You look at me and you see a face that Carl Anthony kissed—Carl, my moment of salvation and freedom. Lord, why can't a moment be forever? Carl Anthony and me fucked in rooms of piss filled toilets and the faint rose scent of Lifebuoy soap in the steamed air. Carl Anthony's solid brown body trembled as if a live current was trickling through him. Our tongues were electric eels that made our cocks rise. I looked at Bully's mouth and felt my lips parting to bite into sweet fruit. Suddenly a blast of cold rushed out of the air vent above me and hit me in the face. I was startled. My revulsion rose up.

"Say Mister, I don't like your soft hand on my arm. And I don't like the feeling it's making me feel. So keep your trouble to yourself."

"Bully, I want a chocolate bar," his Mama pleaded.

"Bully, is they got a toilet in here? I told you I been taking some medicine. I wish y'all hada left me at home."

Bully took his hand off my arm, but kept his knee, which felt like a stone, next to mine. He looked at me with eyes old and cloudy like a long dead trout. He sighed. As his foul breath left him, some invisible force pulled his mouth into a frown. His neck disappeared and his chin sank into his fat chest.

I roll my eyes. get up. brush my ass pocket off, and leave my ass of trouble behind me in that chair. I feel too glad to be free. The hot sun kisses my face when we meet on the other side of the glass door. Then, in all of that warmth I feel a thin cold hand on my wrist. "Bully! Bully!" a voice calls me. I turn and look straight into Mama's quivering face.

Trapped. I am still sitting, hammered and vised between these two old women. Outside through the glass is some other sassy gum-smacking buck tasting freedom. I watch him race across the street, daring the oncoming cars to strike him down. When he gets to the other side, he stuffs his hands in the front pockets of his blue jeans, cocks his head to the side, and takes on this slow I-own-the-world hip swaying walk. I gaze at his back for blocks until heat vapors rise from the sidewalk and consume him. I catch myself feeling ashamed for watching him, wanting him, wishing he could move me backward through my years—fifty, forty, thirty, twenty. I feel foolish for feeling that just a touch of his flesh would propel me back into the arms of Carl Anthony—to taste fire once more. I sit and shiver between these ancient women, while waiting for the clock to stop.

The THING

The soldiers stood waiting impatiently for the sun to shine. They stood next to the THING and bent their yellow flaxen and black woolen heads back. They scanned the sky earnestly. Steel-gray clouds hung low, crushed their spirit. They looked dwarfish. The soldiers spat, cursed, and shifted their feet as if they were grinding ants with their boots. Women soldiers stood with the men, flank to flank. Their uniforms fit them like balloons and gave them hulking shoulders. They cursed louder than the men.

The Civillain* populace stood on the sidelines fanning flies and also watching for the sun. They were eager for a reason to wave their crimson and royal blue flags. They wanted excitement, some kind of violent diversion. Football no longer made their asses twitch in ecstasy. Not even when the players were pitted against wild boars, bulls, or wounded elephants. The Civillains wanted more. They stood on the verge of a whorehouse of an orgasm. Only the shining sun could release this last nut of lust and blood.

"Oh God, let the sun shine

And release the THING to blow

To confetti bits, the enemy."

This was the cry of the Civillains because it was the cry of their Leader. The "enemy" was the people of Psyclops—people similar to them—individuals who ate flesh and roots just as the Civillains. They were people who sometimes ate their children just as the Civillains did. The only difference was that the Civillains had eyes that sparkled like green diamonds. The people of Psyclops had no eyes. What should have been eyes, were pus-filled holes that leaked a thick yellowish liquid.

The Leader of the Civillains knew the value of this liquid. Mixed with pure table salt from a blue box, this substance turned to gold dust. This was the real reason why the THING was aimed at the Psyclopians. They had to be made weak to be captured. Only The THING could penetrate the mile thick excrement shield over the Psyclopian city of Dung Ho. But as for the Civillains cared, all they needed was a diversion to hide their woes from themselves. They didn't give a shit about the gold dust.

They had many woes. However, hunger and a puzzling new disease were the leading Civillain butt kickers. This new disease caused anuses to close. Those stricken, defecated through their mouths. The blessing of the disease was that those who had it and suffered from hunger never knew they were hungry. In fact, if they were fortunate to have the disease, they looked fine and robust until a violent explosion roared from their mouths, and they choked to death on their feces. The hungry Civillains free from the "disease" simply agonized themselves to death. "At least they are full," mocked the hunger sufferers. Just look at their big bellies!"

There was also a lack of burial space for the dead. This fact created new diseases and caused a plague of giant shiny blue flies to descend on the population. The Leader said there was no money to fight the woes of the Civillains. All the money had to be spent to build the THING so they could kill the foul smelling Psyclopians whose eyes were causing the Civillains to be ill. No one spoke up to point out that the Psyclopians had no eyes. To do so meant a penalty of a horrible death. Imagine being boiled in tar and oxtails.

The more the Leader spoke, the more the Civillains hated the Psyclopians, whom they had never seen. Thus, everyone had good reason to stand and wait for the sun to shine. The sun's rays were the key to their survival. The sun was needed to ignite the THING and thus end their woes.

When the commander of the soldiers thought he saw a slice of the honeydew colored sun, he ordered the THING (Thermal Heat Ignition Nuclear Gun) moved to the spot where he thought the sun's rays fell. The flat green truck crept like a stuffed alligator on huge donut wheels. When the vehicle reached its destination with the THING on its back, the sun was not there. The soldiers resumed their sky watching: shifting, grinding, and cursing the clouds.

The THING was a huge pyramid made of three mirrored triangles. It was seven stories high and thirteen hundred feet wide. The THING's hollow contained one hundred rockets. Each rocket carried one thousand mortars. Every mortar swelled with ten thousand shells. One hundred thousand pellets rattled inside of each shell. One pellet was powerful enough to turn an All Right parking lot into a geyser of blue flames. For the THING to work, it was imperative for the sun to shine.

The commanders in deer antler helmets bickered among each other.

"Why couldn't you get a faster truck to move the THING?" General Snutz demanded from General Gast.

"And what idiot ordered airplanes to drop rain capsules on the clouds," retorted Gast. "Look at them clouds gray and heavy with water. And if your intent was to drown the enemy, Sir, why did you drop the pills so close to home? And of course, only a nimble brain like yours would forget the shit dome over the Psyclopians. Seeding clouds! Boo!"

"A faster truck! A faster truck," Gast squealed. The two commanders stood for hours butting each other in anger before another idea hit then in the butt. They decided to use an old sea captain to serve as a lookout for them. (He wasn't really a sea captain. The old man spent fifty years in a touring theatrical production of Moby Dick. He had risen through the ranks from stagehand to member of the chorus line. However, he was patriotic and looked decent in a captain's hat.) The Commanders installed him in a white house high above the base. The old man loved his job too much. He had an uncanny ability to see the sun when it really wasn't there.

"Snutz, Gast, move the THING to the north end of the base! Move it east! There goes the sun, in the west. Hurry! Don't let the blue flies bite you on the ass! Quickly, move the THING." In his quieter moments, he sang an old Beatles tune: *Here comes the sun, Here comes the sun and I say it's alright.*

He drove the commanders and their men crazy. They decided that his zeal might cause considerable damage to the THING. They thanked him for his services and drove him away in a boxy black car adorned with flags and cheerleaders.

The following weeks were filled with blackish gray clouds, shaped like toadstools. And the soldiers walked as if they carried upon their shoulders sacks of lead. The Civillains were not pleased. Many more were belching feces and dying. The commanders, grasping at the last straw, called in a Cardinal.

The Cardinal arrived at the base arrayed in an elegant peacock headdress. His robes shimmered as if they were a golden heat mirage one might see in the desert. His black leather pumps outshined the General's polished hooves. He leaned on a staff of gleaming emeralds. At the crown of his staff was a four-headed python. Inscribed in Latin on this pole were the words, "The Eyes of Man." A young boy in white robes carried a cross and preceded the Cardinal who stopped and kneeled next to the granite typewriter-shaped monument dedicated to "POETS WHO SPEAK AS INSTRUCTED." He touched the ground with his forehead, and the boy marked the spot with the cross. The priest led the commanders and their men in prayer. The women marveled at the pomp and dignity. The men wondered if the Cardinal had the balls to do what needed to be done.

"Oh God, strike dead our eyeless enemy. Rent them from your earth. Confuse their sexuality. Make their men lust after their own sons and their Mothers eat their daughters. Pour bitter sugar down their throats and make their gears grind to a halt. Scud their missiles and make them blow up in their homes. They are dogs! Yes, yes, yes, strike dead our eyeless carrion eaters. May their head Mullah pop his cork. This is our prayer. Your humble servant, your peace-loving vicar of the Godful people of this land. Amen."

After this prayer was uttered and the Cardinal sprinkled the crowd with holy tomato juice, the events that followed made the biblical Day of Pentecost seem like a meeting of stamp collectors. Flaming eagles screamed across the sky. Doves swelled with violence and tore giant anacondas from the Amazon. The money-changers in the House of Morgan and Chase opened their windows and threw gold out into the street. They then ran to the ocean and drowned. The seas bobbed with fat bellies and the sharks who loved them. The Civillains so overcome, could only fall to their knees and beat the ground. Even the soldiers trembled. Suddenly the clouds parted, and the sun shot an arrow of light that blazed upon on the THING. Then the sun's rays rained down in sparkling cascades of lights.

The soldiers cheered, and some fell on their knees, thanking their God. A flag was raised. They saluted it with tears in their eyes. The commanders raved how great and brave they were, and how the world would thank them for freedom. The old sea captain was brought back. They had not forgotten his zeal. He preached, stuffing them with words of their goodness and planted this idea that swelled in them, "Armed freedom is better than life without eyes." He suggested to the Cardinal that they form a partnership to promote the ideas that only people with emerald eyes be allowed to vote and have windows in their homes.

As the sun's rays burned the giant mirrors of the THING, it cracked from the heat and spat its massive rockets toward the Psyclopians. The soldiers and Civillains were filled with a black rapture. Blood rushed to their faces, colored them a dark purple, and burst their brains through their ears. This syrup drowned them and thus ended their woes. The Psyclopians who were supposed to die, never felt a damn thing except a hot flash, which the women blamed on menopause. The THING lies at the bottom of a Martian sea this very day.

*Civillain is the correct spelling for the characters in The THING.

Happy

John Wayne dressed in a gold wig, white chiffon gown, and oversized cowboy boots, puckered his red lips at the boy dressed in black cowhide chaps and silver studs. After a night of loving the boy (licking his inner thighs and nibbling his ankles) John Wayne in a fit of schizophrenia became his old enigmatic self, took a Colt-45 and shot off the bag that held the boy's jewels. He then placed that boy's manhood on a makeshift altar of burning candles and dung.

"Now you will see," said John Wayne, "There is good in suffering. You will sit here and write poetry the rest of your life. You will become famous and rich. Women will love you. Capote and Tennessee will turn over in their graves with envy."

So the boy wrote:

My manhood rots

in the garden

of cabbage leaves.

Where children once grew

yellow fat drips

and splatters my thighs.

My hips are big as money bags

and heavy with gold

I am suffering.

I am happy.

The boy carved those words into John Wayne's skull and chiseled them into his breastbone, which he refused to bury. "I will never forget my happiness and neither shall he," he said pointing at John Wayne's hollow eye sockets.

Journalists gathered at the boy's feet like anxious cats waiting on fish guts. Microphones crackled like lightning. Pens spilled blood ink. Suddenly a voice shouted, "Get on board the Burlington Northern. They're cooking niggers in a Milwaukee chocolate factory!"

The boy cried out as one would do if they were being boiled alive and grabbed after the coattails of the fleeing journalists. They shook him loose like a cat shakes off life number five.

The boy sat and cried red tears. Another mad poet had stolen his thunder.

###

Charity

Gusta lay in the middle of the four corners of Main Street with his black ulcerated leg opened and oozing gray. Two ladies in tweed suits and puffed hair, stepped gingerly over him. They stood next to Gusta's leg and chattered over dog jewelry, black caviar, and the daring Japanese Kamikaze Ballet that killed each other with swords night after night. During their discourse, a gold tooth fell from one of the women's gums and landed on Gusta's leg. The gold reacted harshly to the grayish substance that seeped from his wound. He died after a day of agony. A talking horse claimed to have seen Gusta at the racetrack. This turned out to be a lie. However folks still hold onto the hope of Gusta's life.

In the meantime, flies came in droves. They washed their legs in Gusta's oozing sores. So many flies came. The late comers crushed those already at the trough of Gusta's body. More came and crushed those who had had been crushed.

A scientist announced that many of the flies were from the jungles of Africa, and their emerald colored wings were worth more than gold. The rich women became alarmed and quickly formed a charity to save the flies. They took off their tweed jackets and silk blouses and squeezed their nipples until all the creamy milk ran out. However their milk was too rich, and all of the flies died. Gusta's body was burdened with dead flies and too much charity. Too heavy to lift, they let him rot in the hot sun and freeze in the winter snow until he was all gone. The women received gold medals for their kindness from popes and presidents.

###

The Cicadas Have Landed

As Mabel Marie bounced through the smoky doors of the LaSalle Building, a cicada landed in the uppermost region of her tall hair. And when I say tall hair, I mean Texas-sized hair with blond locks where the bees get lightheaded flying in and around the hive. A mute in a tattered coat and missing his fingers on his right hand, except his middle finger, pointed and sputtered at her head. He sprinkled Mabel Marie's blue suit coat with spittle. She reciprocated with a rude gesture. His face turned purple, and he stabbed at her furiously with his one finger.

"You too, buddy," Mabel Marie said as she continued down New Hampshire Avenue. She dug in her handbag and found a wad of Kleenex and dabbed her sleeve. She looked around as she crossed Constitution. The man stared at her. Mabel Marie kept on down the street. She wondered whether the Director was somehow mixed up in this nuttiness. He was the kind of man who would stoop as low as a Texas rattlesnake, Mabel Marie thought.

"Rattlesnakes!" Mabel stopped all of a sudden. She looked down at her feet. No, she was not in a pit of snakes in a swamp in east Texas. But where in the heck was that noise like a cauldron of boiling snakes coming from. She looked toward the sky. The clouds were gray as cat fur and moved in motion as if a giant hand was painting over the sun. Then she heard what sounded like someone snapping string beans and felt a thump on her arm. Suddenly, Mabel Marie saw cicadas hovering near her nose and felt them beating her shoulders. They flew in droves. Bushes and trees burdened with their bodies shimmered like gray glass. The air hissed. "Else if thou refuse to let my people go, behold, to morrow I will bring the locust in thy coast." Words from her pastor's sermon played in Mabel's head. She likened the cicadas to locusts and blamed that "horrible pharaoh" Bill Clinton. "You can't trust anyone to tell you the time of day truthfully these days," Mabel thought. She passed a newspaper stand full of gaudy tabloids with screaming headlines: "**DEVIL IN A BLUE DRESS ... I CAN TELL A LIE ... HILLARY BUSTS BILL'S BALLS ...**" She looked up at the George Washington Monument and sighed. "At least you didn't tell a lie, Georgie."

Her week at the office had been a weird one. The number 666 appeared like stigmata in pale red on all of her reports. Tech Support said the only way to get rid of it was to wipe clean her hard drive. "Clean as a bald headed Japanese," Arnold said behind his horn-rimmed glasses. She reminded him that most Japanese had hair these days. Mabel felt the Director's hot blue eyes on her back, but when she turned around to face him, he thrust his nose into a sheaf of papers or out the window toward the capitol whose dome out-shined his. Her lunches disappeared from the refrigerator.

"Sue Crossley," Mabel said aloud. "Maybe I can get the truth from her. Then I can give The Director a good Texas ass whipping."

The façade of the Filibuster Restaurant loomed before her like an enormous red brick barbecue pit. In front of the restaurant, the United States flag waved as if it was being carried into battle. Mabel marched on, crunching cicadas under her flats.

She reached the Filibuster and pushed through its massive vault-like doors. She gazed up at the portraits of past Speakers of the House and didn't recognize a single name—though she thought one jowly face that had snoozed during Lyndon Johnson's State of the Union Speech looked familiar. Mabel remembered how that Texas twang had comforted her as she sat listening to it leaning against her grandmother's swollen legs. "Lord," she thought, "I can use those legs and Texas twang right about now. Life in Washington ain't no crystal stair."

Mabel spoke to the Maitre D', and he pointed to a table under a portrait of a tight-lipped George Washington. Sue Crossley rose and shook Mabel Marie's hand as if Mabel was a client, though they worked in the same department at The LaSalle Institute for Political Action and had seen one another moments earlier. Mabel bumped the silverware as she sat. Sue paused before taking her seat. Something shiny on top of Mabel Marie's hair caught her eye. She squinted for a second, smiled at Mabel, and sat down.

"The cicadas are murder this season," Sue said as she brushed her fingers through her blond pageboy. The ends curled into a conch shell. Her hair reminded Mabel of America's Founding Fathers. Mabel trusted Sue.

"Not to mention the nuts walking the streets," Mabel countered. "Some idiot out of the blue comes up to me, gives me the finger, and spits all over me."

"My goodness. Two Cosmopolitans." Sue raised two fingers and whispered to a Waiter hovering nearby.

"Oh!" Mabel looked startled. "Are we putting drinks on the expense account?" She looked straight at Sue. Though Mabel Marie was Project Lead and Sue was a Receptionist Grade Three, Sue didn't blink an eye.

"We work for LaSalle. We can buy the restaurant, Dear."

"It's just my first time here and..."

"Trust me." A loud clattering noise was heard from the kitchen. It garbled Sue's words.

"Excuse me," Mabel frowned.

"I said, you can trust me."

Mabel Marie broke out in heaving guffaws. The cicada bounced with her catching glints of gold from the restaurant's chandelier in its membranous wings. Sue stared at her. Mabel's laughter receded to a series of small hiccups.

"I thought you said 'you can fuck me.' I was thinking to myself this day is stranger than fiction."

"I only get fucked at the office, Dear."

The grin dissolved from Mabel's face. She looked at Sue for a moment then laughed quietly. "Yes, I know what you mean."

The waiter brought the Cosmopolitans. The red color in the drinks matched the stone in the large class ring on his pinky finger. The inscription in block letters read GWU 1999. Mabel bit one of her fingernails and looked away.

"Nice restaurant," Mabel said looking about at various US history motifs. A stuffed bald eagle with outstretched wings acted as sentry to a dark room in the rear of the Filibuster. Mabel barely made out the dusty light from the far-away chandelier. She looked at other diners hunched over, whispering quietly, and dabbing at their lips with napkins.

"The cream of the crop," Sue winked.

"Is the food here any good?"

"Food is food. The Filibuster is about seeing who goes underneath the eagle's wings."

"I don't understand."

"Seeing who's who, Dear."

"Oh. Oh! I get it. That must be a very important room." Mabel and the cicada nodded toward the eagle. Sue smiled and nibbled on a roll. She put it down.

"You sounded worried when you asked me to meet you for lunch."

Mabel took a sip of her cosmopolitan. A piece of lime stuck to her upper lip. She felt it and flicked her tongue upward to remove it. The gesture reminded Sue of her mother, who flicked her tongue across her top lip after she blew smoke from her cigarette.

"Do you smoke?" Sue asked.

"No, never. I wish no one smoked."

"Well, some idiots do. And it's our job to make sure Phillip Morris keeps them lighting up."

Mabel looked wide-eyed at Sue as if Sue had cursed her.

"Sue, I think…" Mabel cocked her head and frowned. "I keep hearing a faint chirping noise." She dug into her purse and scooped out her cell phone. A piece of duct tape swung from the bottom of it. A hair roller clung to the tape. Sue frowned. Mabel yanked the roller off and looked at the phone. She hunched her shoulders and put the phone back in her purse.

"Sue, they have enough tar in their cigarettes to pave a Texas highway. And that road is littered with the bones of cancer victims."

"Let's hope it's not littered with the bones of a particular Project Lead," Sue said as she picked up a menu.

Mabel Marie banged her fist on the table. "I knew it. I knew it. I knew it. That bastard is out for my blood."

"He's out for your ass, Dear."

"Sue, lung cancer killed my Grandfather."

"It killed my Mother, but what's lung cancer got to do with you showing more leg?"

"I beg your pardon?"

"You're spooking the Director."

"Spooking him? What do you mean?"

"You're so serious. Raise the hemline a little."

"And that will get the Director off my ass—walking around like a floozy? I've been a Project Lead for Ad agencies and PR firms for years. 'Milk, it does the body good,' that's mine. If it weren't for me, it would have been 'Milk does good.' Imagine how lame that would have been."

"'You've come a long way, baby.'" Sue winked at Mabel. "Are you ready to order?" Sue picked up the red, white, and blue menu and scanned it. Mabel picked up her menu, glanced at it, and put it down.

"That 'long way, baby' has caused women's cancer deaths to come within twenty percentage points of men's. But wiggle your ass, Mabel Marie, and the world at LaSalle is all right."

"Look, Mabel, The Director likes strong women, but he doesn't want them looking like grandmothers tromping behind an ox-cart. It doesn't hurt a woman..." Sue paused and looked at Mabel Marie. "Let me put it this way. At LaSalle, a woman is expected to be a bitch and get the job done. Take off your angel wings and put on the devil's cape. When you leave work tonight, stop by Saks and pick out a couple of Oscar De La Renta suits and a pair of Bruno Frisonis. Think of fire when you shop—reds, oranges, cool blues," Sue growled and pawed the air as she rattled off the colors. "In the morning go toe to toe with the man. By that evening, swayed by your charm he may cancel the Phillip Morris contract, and we can all go stand in the unemployment line."

Before Mabel could respond, Sue threw her hand in the air, and the waiter stepped over. "I'll have the Caesar with buttermilk dressing—good for your skin," she winked at Mabel, "grilled shark over roasted vegetables, and for dessert a chocolate martini—Oh! She'll have the same." Sue slapped her menu shut. The tulips in the centerpiece fluttered. Mabel sat frowning.

"No. No. No," she murmured.

Sue and the waiter looked at Mabel. The waiter slowly withdrew his hand from Mabel's menu. Mabel looked up at the portrait of George Washington as if seeking moral support.

"That's too expensive. The budget for LaSalle is my responsibility."

The waiter moved in closer to look at the thing in Mabel's hair. Sue cleared her throat and he stepped back.

"I'll just have the garden salad and tonic water. She smiled at Mabel. "After all, you're the boss."

"I'm not the boss. I'm only responsible for the budget—even though..."

"The man is waiting, Dear." Sue nodded toward the waiter.

"Tuna salad and water."

Sue took a sip of what was left of her cosmopolitan. She slyly glanced at the cicada as if it were a co-conspirator. A herd of men in dark suits drifted through the Filibuster. As they passed behind Mabel, one looked into her hair. He looked over at Sue, who put her finger to her lips as if she were scratching her nose. The man smiled and slid his hand across his throat imitating a knife blade. By the time Mabel turned to see the commotion behind her, the men were moving toward the eagle.

"Who are they?" Mabel asked. "They look important."

"Just flunkies from another firm." Sue looked at Mabel and smiled.

Mabel Marie eyed the men suspiciously as they glided under the eagle's outstretched wings. An army of waiters bearing silver platters across their chests like shields stepped quickly and disappeared into the room behind them. "'Some 'flunkies' indeed," she said to herself. As she turned to face Sue, the Filibuster's Maître D' placed a small sign near the entry to the room where the men dined. It read: PHILLIP MORRIS EXECUTIVE COMMITTEE. Mabel did not see the sign.

"So Mabel do you miss your PR job in Tennessee?"

"Texas. And yes I miss it. I miss the Texas hills and my Grandma Rose's pecan pies. She'd be up all night baking, then sleep the next day as the pies cooled under her glass showcase. All a customer had to do was just walk in and leave two dollars in a pickle jar while she snoozed."

"She trusted people like that?"

"Of course, besides Miss Beulah sat on her porch across the street eyeing everybody and everything that went in-and-out Grandma's house."

"It must be a pain for you to work at a place like LaSalle," Sue said. "The values of LaSalle are all talk. 'We love our clients better than we love our Mothers.' Nonsense from one of the most backstabbing joints in DC" Sue leaned forward averting her eyes from the cicada. "Thank God you got there on the tail end of 'Genesis.'"

"Genesis—the Indian Casino Lobby effort?"

"No, Dear, Geronimo was the Indian Casino Lobby. Genesis was the Christian lobby effort, God's Genesis Against Gambling—GGAG."

"Double-dipping."

"At LaSalle, the requirement for new employees is that they learn to speak out of both sides of their mouths at once."

"Wow."

"They're in bed with Coal Miners and Coal mine owners; anti-abortionists and pro-abortionists; the AFL-CIO and Global Works, one of the biggest outsourcing firms in the country. We should change our motto from 'We hold our friends by the hand' to 'We hold our friends and their enemies in the same claws.' Does that sound like Texas values to you?"

"Sounds like a pit of Texas rattlers. Worse than a snake. A snake will only bite once."

"That's how the Director wants things. Small town girls in long dresses who look like Mothers make him nervous. He keeps a picture of that Watkins woman who spilled the beans about Enron in the center of his dart board."

Mabel sat with a stricken face. "Maybe I should quit."

"Aw now, Mabel" Sue glanced at the cicada and smiled to herself. The waiter brought their lunches and busily arranged the table as if setting up a five-course meal. As he worked, Mabel looked at his ring. When he left, she spoke up.

"That guy, he graduated from Georgetown, and he's waiting tables."

"Perhaps he has small minded values too." Sue minced at her salad.

A flash of pink lit Mabel's face like a neon sign. She picked up her fork then put it down.

"I signed off on that last piece of Genesis budget. I noticed you received a large bonus, Sue."

"And your point is?"

"My point is..." Mabel snapped her neck to look Sue straight in the eyes. The cicada landed in her salad and vibrated its wings furiously. It sounded like a dozen crickets chirping. Faces from other tables turned in Mabel's direction.

"Has that been in my hair all this time?"

"I don't know. I wasn't looking at your hair that much."

"It was, and you know it was."

"I thought it was a little doodad hair decoration from Texas."

"How did you know about my problem with the Phillip Morris Account? You said earlier when I talked about cancer bones littering the highway, 'Let's hope it's not a Project Lead's bones.' You know the Director is after me. You know it!"

"I don't know what you mean, girl?"

"Girl?"

"Don't make me say worse," Sue growled low like a cat ready to pounce. "You, the 'Savior of LaSalle' with your big hair watching over budgets like a Texas hen. LaSalle expects us to spend its money, not go out and eat like sparrows." Sue raised her hand. The waiter came quickly to the table. "Take this rabbit food back and bring me a steak and a Bloody Mary."

"I will not approve that expense, Sue."

"You will approve it because the Director will approve it, girl. Yes, the Director is after your blood and not your fat ass."

The word "ass" assaulted sensitive ears in the entire restaurant. A spoon stirred nervously in a glass of iced tea. Sue's attack continued.

"Your nit-picking over this and that and your goddamned principles—Don't you know anything about how the world runs circles around your ass? You're born and the people who make diapers get a piece of your ass. Then it's Toys R Us' turn. You grow up to buy cars, clothes, and goddamn chicken for your pot. And do you think that chicken jumps in your pot straight from some grandpa's farm? Ugly things have to be done to get the chicken into three-hundred-million mouths, girl—things that fuck up rivers and the air sometimes. So what if Phillip Morris causes cancer. Cancer fills hospitals—gives Doctors, Nurses, and floor scrubbers something to do. Then you die, and the undertakers get the last piece of your ass..."

Mabel rose from her chair. Sue stood also. She yelled the last four digits of LaSalle's account to the waiter. He bowed as the women passed. Sue nipped after Mabel, who plowed ahead with her head pushed into her shoulders as if she had swallowed herself.

"LaSalle's duty is to make sure the circle doesn't get broken by mindless do-gooders with so-called principles. I'm just a cog in the wheel at LaSalle. LaSalle is one of many wheels turning this world round and round every day. My mom died of cancer. Killing Phillip Morris ain't gonna bring her back. And it sure as hell ain't gonna stop nobody from smoking. You fuck with the Director and our biggest account, you'll be the one pushing up daisies."

Mabel Marie pushed her neck up and turned to Sue. "At least when I die, I will go to heaven."

"Oh, child," Sue scoffed, "Is that all you got?"

Mabel Marie marched down Constitution Avenue as the cicadas beat their wings in her ears and Sue's hot breath heated her neck. In a moment, the women found themselves in front of a small boutique. The female mannequins posed with their noses in the air and sported women suits with ties. Mabel turned and looked at Sue. She didn't know why she did it, but she grabbed a handful of Sue's hair. The George Washington do lifted off without a struggle and there stood Sue as bald as Capitol Hill. The cicadas drawn to her shiny dome descended like locusts.

####

Mabel's Elephant Problem

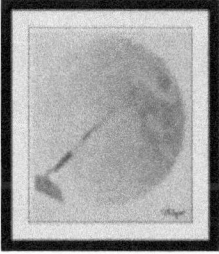

I hate to lie, but lying is necessary for survival in these days and times. Sue calls herself a gourmet cook and being high up in the government she gets away with anything. She came calling, and you'll never guess what that heifer brought—a banana and lamb chop casserole. I smiled and said, "How nice," as Sue plopped herself on my old couch.

I took the casserole and put it on the stove. I had eaten, and I'd fed Harry. It was kind of nice to have a visitor. I was rocking a new turban. Sue admired it and asked if I was a Turbanasian. I thanked her for liking the fake rubies and emeralds sewn into that scratchy woolyester fabric made from lab cloned sheep—a government concoction of course. My turban rose high in swirls like soft scoop ice cream. Or you can just close your eyes and imagine me with a conch shell on my head sprinkled with jewels walking along the Nile going, "bah baaah baaah." Of course, the Nile is not surrounded by a beach. There would be no conch shell. And the lab-cloned sheep are as silent as slugs. But I think we're still allowed some imagination, so imagine. Sue looked around the room at my various pieces of castoff furniture. I'm certain she had her electronic eye scanning the barcodes to see if my furniture was newer than ten years. At my level, I'm not allowed to have anything newer than ten years. Satisfied that my crap was vintage 2001 stuff, she smiled and opened that trap of hers to make conversation.

"So how do you like the new flag, Mabel?" There was a clattering in her jaws like her teeth were loose and large pieces of platinum were rolling between her cheeks.

I cleared my throat and thought before I answered. A wrong answer in this day and age could get you sent before the Three Judges and on to the Lobotomy Lab. Harry would testify to that if he could.

"Well, I understand the hoe symbolizes hard work. But I don't know why they have it stuck in the moon like that?"

"You don't think the hoe should be stuck in the moon?" Sue gazed at me with that one brilliantly electronic blue eye. The bouncy letters of the latest news feed skipped in front of her gray eye. She had no doubt turned on her recorder for sure.

"Oh heavens yes! The hoe looks great stuck in the moon. But I thought the President said they were going to stick the hoe in Mars."

"Oh, you really should keep up with the news, Mabel."

"Our telepad is broken."

Sue looked over at my telepad pad hanging from the wall by its one rabbit ear antennae. She shook her head and patted my hand. "I'll see what I can do."

I prayed that wasn't a threat. Everyone is supposed to have a working telepad to receive government broadcasts and to watch the cooking shows. At my level, all I'm allowed are the old Julia Child reruns. I can make Coq au Vin in my sleep, though folks at my rank aren't authorized to eat it. I'm sure they must serve the cock at those decadent upper-level government parties. Hmmm.

Having a broken telepad could lead them to dye my eyes a hideous yellow. This new government has some very creative punishments—from making you get strange tattoos to cutting your tongue out. And they're like stink on rotten cabbage. You can't get away from them. They've installed cameras in closets and bathrooms and employ elderly women to sit and stare at us all day, and write in their little notebooks. We had an "Elder" here up until last month when she passed away. She's now mummifying under a pile of 1970's Look Magazines in the hall closet. We're still waiting on the body collectors. I've called those folks and called those folks. I gave up after pressing "pound sixty-nine" one hundred times on the iPodphonius*.

Sue's roving eyes landed on Harry. She sighed, "Poor Harry."

"You telling me," I said. "He's just a big lump. Nobody recognizes him anymore."

Sue waved at Harry like you wave at someone to see if they're blind. Harry stared straight ahead.

"He wasn't always so, so, so shy. What happened?"

Shy? I hid my anger at her stupidity with a loud laugh. How could she of all people not know what happened to my Harry? She's married to a 15.1C, a big cheese who works in the Government Information office. But just in case, this Sue creature was dangerous, I started telling the story of Harry's near demise, telling as much as I could, as best I could. I wasn't taking any chances with this weird cooker of bananas.

"I was washing my dishes according to the instructions in the manual. Those things are so silly. Even though we had had beef broth and crackers for lunch, I still had to wash each bowl with the rekwired one hundred strokes. I couldn't cut it short at say ninety-nine strokes. The camera is aimed right at my sink. It's broken today."

Sue looked at the huge eyeball revolving on a silver stem. When it's live, it has the aura of a dreamy-eyed movie star. In its broken state, it has all the personality of a boiled egg Julia has set aside for tuna salad.

"We, I mean you, must get that fixed right away. A broken eyecam generally triggers a SWAT alert. I'm surprised we aren't surrounded by men pointing their penises at us...pointing their penises at us...pointing..."

I went over and slapped Sue's ear. That dislodged her tongue. "Pointing their guns at us," she corrected herself.

"Well if you look across the street at the Murphy's you'll see SWAT all over the place."

Sue craned her neck toward the window. Sure enough, SWAT had their weapons aimed at a bewildered Mr. and Mrs. Murphy, who crawled on their stomachs. "Well so much for government efficiency," Sue said. Then she sat up abruptly like some kind of hunting dog who got a whiff of a raccoon or prison escapee. "Mabel, I noticed your doorbell didn't whoop when I buzzed."

"The Whooper is broken."

"Broken? Girl, you are indeed off the grid. But don't worry. I won't breathe this to a soul."

"Thanks, Sue. You are so kind." I wondered to myself if a magnetic screwdriver to the eye would screw up her neuronic circuitry. Or perhaps some L'oreal Advanced Hairstyle TXT IT Deconstructing Gum could muck up the antennae in that fake blond hair. To get my mind off of wicked thoughts, I brought up the doorbell rules.

"And that's another one of these strange rules I don't understand. Ipodphonious's and doorbells in private domiciles must whoop. Only the ones in government offices can ring!"

"It's the General's wife. She has a thing for Whooping Cranes and Koala Bears. If your telepad was working you'd know these things," Sue said in singsong teasing voice which did little to reassure me she wasn't mocking me and using her neuronic circuitry to plot my punishments. Women like Sue are dangerous. I'm sure there was some kind of recorder in that roving eye of hers.

"Well, at least the whooper was working that day the postman rang it," I said in my defense. "Harry got up and answered the door. I would have answered it myself, but I didn't want to stop washing dishes. I was in the middle of the fiftieth stroke on Harry's bowl, and I hadn't even started mine. Then I heard Harry sputter. 'No. No, I am not speaking against the government, but I did not order an elephant!' When Harry sputters, he sprays, you know, spits. By the time I got to the door, the postman was moderately sprinkled. That was trouble enough for Harry. Do you remember the woman with the cerebral palsy who spilled ink on the floor of the Entitlements Office?"

Sue cocked her head like a poodle as she tried to recall. I knew good and darn well Sue knew whom I was talking about. She was the one who pointed out the poor soul to the Government goons. But I carried on as if Sue was an empty vessel that needed filling. To be frank, it was nice to have someone to talk to, even if the conversation might land you before the three judges. What can one say to an elephant except, "Mish, mish, mish," as you guide her around the pen with a stick and hope the cow doesn't step on your foot. "Mish" works just as well with Harry too.

"No. What happened to that poor dear soul?" Sue's tone was condescending and syrupy as if I was a giant fly she was trying to bait.

"They took her to the hospital and cut off her lips. They even took the bridge out of her nose. Now her face looks as flat as an iron. And there stood poor Harry spotting the postman's uniform. He kept saying, 'I did not order an elephant!'"

"You know our address is 1121 Lincoln, and the Zoo's is 1211 Lincoln. I had told Harry that I did not like living so close to the zoo. But he prevailed since it was near his job."

"Men and their jobs!" Sue beat her fist against the couch cushion.

"Hmm," I said to myself. "It must not be so hot being married to a 15.1C after all, even if you're allowed to shop for onions at Carmichael's Onion Emporium where their sweet onions are 'sweet enough to stop an elephant's tears.'"

Sorry for that commercial interruption. The government has decreed that all conversations have at least one commercial—anything to raise revenue. Sue continued to beat the couch cushion. She had become stuck again. There's something wrong with this woman's wiring, I said to myself as I slapped her left breast. I think that's where the controls in Humanoids reside for bodily motion. If you remember earlier, I hit her ear when her speech locked up. When I first met Sue a few months back, I thought she was a real woman, the kind made of flesh and blood like me. I found out later she's one of those mechanical women this new government awards to their upper echelon men.

When Sue stopped beating the couch, she asked me what Harry used to do for a living. "Surely they've wired this bitch with more than eight gigabits of memory," I thought to myself. The President's wife has sixteen terabits in her large head. She looks adorable in hats. The last First Lady, who wore a hat, was Jackie Kennedy, I think. Perhaps her husband should have worn the hat. Might have confused that Lee Harvey fella. But I better entertain Sue's question. She might be testing my ability to recall. If you're unable to recall the events of your life, the government changes your sex. We've become a mecca for European transsexuals pretending to have amnesia.

"My Harry had a good job at the Government Press Office," I continue. "He was a proofreader. He combed the newspapers in search of words that began with the letter Q."

"Q is a bad letter," Sue said studying her fingernails. The government is right to try and purge it from the language."

"I guess it's that little tail thing that looks like a pig's tail."

"It's death to anyone who calls a government official a pig. And rightfully so. We are aardvarks and anteaters, not pigs!"

"So true," I said trying to sound as patriotic as Sue. But for the life of me, I didn't understand why this new government liked being called aardvarks or anteaters.

When Harry was working, he came home with a little aardvark figurine given to him for an exemplary achievement at work. He got it for catching the letter Q with the tail switched to the left. A subversive was trying to get a message to a Turbanasian in the penal colony. But Harry caught that left tailed Q and received a Golden Aardvark for his work. One night as I massaged his toes, I asked him what was so special about the aardvark. He shrugged and smiled at the little figurine on the bookshelf propping up our banned copy of Wallington's *The Uke of Wallington—One Man and his Ukulele Around Britain*. I had guessed the General's wife has a hatred of the ukulele. Harry could get away with having banned novels on the bookshelf. Banned books were part of his work.

"We are first in everything!" Sue shouted and pointed her finger toward the ceiling.

"Oh yes, we are," I said meekly. "First," I repeated. Now it made sense as I thought of the little dictionary my Grandmother use to have on her bookshelf next to her false teeth. The first word in it was aardvark. The last word was federalism. She wasn't making any kind of political statement. Her schnauzer had gotten hold of the paperback and chewed off quite a few pages.

"But Sue," and I had to tread carefully because I was stating an opinion. This new government hates ideas. People with opinions get tortured to death by the dreaded foot tickler, which is really a monkey dressed in a King Kong suit. Don't ask. "But Sue, we spend all those billions turning quits to kwits and quests to kwests. No wonder the rest of the world calls us kweer."

"Let them kall us kweer as long as we are korrect."

"I guess so," I said with a bit of uncertainty. I was watching Sue's speech bubble and wondering why she was spelling with a K words that began with C. You're only supposed to do that with words that actually start with a Q. If one could see my speech bubble, they'd see that I did it correctly, not korrectly. Oh, I'm so smart sometimes. I would slap my knee if that weren't against the law.

I noticed Sue had begun to munch the ends of her hair near her mouth. Perhaps If I continued my story, she would eat the wires, recording our conversation.

"Anyway," I continued my story about the elephant, "Harry tried to point out to the postman that our address was 1121 and not 1211. The carrier pointed to the tag on the elephant's rump that said:

ZOO

1121 Lincoln Ave.

Kwadrant 4

District S

Subdivision 10

Section 11.

I liked it much better when we were simply 1121 Lincoln, Indianapolis Indiana, 60059. But you know, government efficiency comes first. Harry said to the man, 'Does this look like a zoo? This is a duplex house assigned to me by the government.'"

"The postman insisted it was his sworn duty to leave packages at the correct address. And he again pointed to the tag on the elephant's rump and the one above our door. The man thrust the pen into Harry's hand for him to sign for the elephant. Harry, of course, being as clever as he is—I mean was, pointed out to the postman that the elephant being so big and unruly, might damage the house and lawn, and in effect would be damaging government property, and he the postman could get into serious trouble. The elephant had already yanked a hedge by the roots and was shaking it like something mad."

"Oh yes! Oh yes! Give mama all of that cock, you bastard! Oh yes! Make me cream, you Mother Fucker!"

I watched as Sue ground and gyrated on the couch. She whimpered, moaned, and grabbed tufts of the chenille coverlet by the fringes. Her eyes walled back in her head. Then she sighed. I watched her breathe and pant as if she had just run a marathon. After a moment, she opened her eyes, crossed her legs and dug into her purse for a cigarette. She took a puff and blew circles that looked like the Olympic rings. "Yes, yes, yes," she sighed.

"Men are so silly. If we aren't allowed to have pets, why would anyone accept an elephant?" She asked as if she had suddenly come back to earth. A condom appeared in her mouth. She chewed and blew it up like a girl chewing bubble gum.

"Uh, that's a good point, Sue. If we aren't allowed cats and dogs, why on earth would anyone send us an elephant?" Sue kept chewing the rubber. Her face had that after sex glow. I kept on telling the story. This new government prefers we be oblivious to things.

"It should not have been delivered to our house. Harry and I didn't think of the cat and dog argument. Anyway the postman—he was Negroid—wrinkled his narrow forehead and appeared to be in deep thought. I thought Harry had got him. But I guess this fellow was full of mother wit, and he pointed out to Harry that the elephant was addressed to ZOO, 1121 Lincoln, you know, Kwadrant blah blah blah blah. And since he the postman was acting in the capacity of deliverer, the elephant was the responsibility of the receiver. There was no way in hell, he said, he could get into trouble if the elephant damaged government property. Even the elephant had to raise her trunk and trumpet at this line of reasoning. Then Harry turned to me."

"'Mabel, did you order this damned thing?'" He was so angry he looked cross-eyed.

Me, being the cautious one said rather timidly that I did not order the elephant, but would be glad to keep it when Harry abruptly cut me off.

"'There, my wife did not order the elephant, and I did not order him ... No, I don't care what the address says. You have made a mistake. No, I am not speaking against the government. I am only saying, Mister...'"

While I was talking, I noticed a strand of Sue's hair sticking straight up. I didn't pay it too much attention. I assumed it was from the pseudo orgasm she had just had. Plus the chenille coverlets are known to throw off enough static electricity to power a toaster. But other hairs began to stand up one by one. I stopped talking long enough to notice Sue's lips trembled as if she was speaking. The hairs then pointed to the Murphy's across the street.

"This witch!" I thought to myself. I've been talking too much. I've got a broken telepad, and my whooper is on the fritz. She's trying to communicate to the Government soldiers across the street to come and arrest me It's a trip for me to the Lobotomy Lab for sure. I had to try and get Sue to redirect the men. I thought of slapping her ear again. But that could set off an alarm of some kind. I could have put an open Bible in front of her. But, then I remembered she was humanoid not vampire. I needed something to block the signal in her hair. I scratched my head and felt my turban. "Ah Hah!" I maneuvered close to Sue.

"I was just thinking what a cute outfit you have on. I love the purple and royal blue swirls. It reminds me of blueberry ice cream. It needs this turban!"

I pulled off my turban and aimed for her head.

"No. No!" she tried to protest. I jammed the hat over her locks and peeped out the window. A soldier cocked his head. He held up his arm. He barked some kind of command and pounded his chest. Suddenly, The Murphy's were crawling back toward their domicile. Confusion took over. Some of the soldiers pointed their guns at each other, while others danced with one another. I did it. I had jammed Sue's communication circuitry. But I knew that wouldn't be enough. She would have to join the "Elder" in the closet.

"Your story! Your Story," Sue shouted. She tugged at the turban. A blond hair sprouted out and aimed at the window toward the Murphy's.

"We were naked," I shouted into Sue's ear.

"You were not naked," Sue yelled back.

"Harry was naked, I mean the postman, the goddamn elephant was naked."

I looked out the window. The soldiers were removing their uniforms.

"Good," I thought. I'm controlling them through Sue. One soldier reminded me of Mel Gibson. I wondered if he was the one giving Sue her pseudo sex fit. Gosh, I sure could use one of those soldiers for my needs.

"You were not naked. There was no one naked in this story."

I looked down. Sue held a small Taser 1000 Derringer.

"Now you get this monkey hat off my head and continue your story, or I will fry your liver."

I did as Sue commanded. I removed the hat from her head and sat it on the table. I wish it were as magical as it looked. Sue pointed her derringer. I picked up where I had left off

"The postman interrupted Harry and asked him how in the world could he make a mistake when he had instructions to deliver all mail to its destination, and that the elephant's tag said 1121 blah blah blah and the address on the house was blah blah blah blah blah! I said to myself, there goes that darned mother wit again. Harry was flustered..."

By now all of Sue's hairs, even her bangs were standing straight up in the air. Her hair resembled angel hair pasta. She was communicating big time. The General himself was probably assembling an assault force to take me down. I was Mabel Sanger, a subversive who remembered too much and questioned idiot government rules. I wished the pipes would burst as they are prone to do in these government bungalows and send water crashing down on that hair of hers. Where is a pot of boiling water when you need it? I looked out the window. The soldiers stood stark naked and confused. They aimed their guns at the Murphy's transport vehicle—a 1998 Impala fitted with heliwings so it could fly. Mr. Murphy now free, grabbed some mail out of his box and slammed the door behind him and Helen. At least the soldiers were still confused. The turban had done some damage to Sue's communication abilities.

"Some of my banana and lamb chop casserole will go well with this story," Sue said gesturing toward the kitchen.

"Perhaps it would." I agreed. I had forgotten about Sue's concoction. In fact, my goal when she delivered it, was to avoid eating it at all costs. But now I saw it as a way it to render her hair as useless as spaghetti.

I set a saucer of casserole in front of Sue and sat down across from her and began to eat mine. I'm good at controlling my gag reflex—very necessary with this dish. Sue picked up her fork and shoveled some into her mouth. Of course, she didn't chew. It was more like she shoved it down her gullet. I wondered how she might be digesting her food. I soon heard a whirring and clacking like a blender grinding up ice. A little puff of smoke seeped from Sue's left ear. My question was answered. Sue picked up her derringer.

"You have such a marvelous memory. Continue your story."

"But it is an elephant! Harry protested. The postman said it was not his job to kwestion people's mail. He said that inspectors had wondered why we were receiving an elephant. But, since it was not a dog or cat, they gave him the OK to deliver the package to 1121 Lincoln. Despite the fact, the name said, "Zoo." He also stated that they had been proactive and took the precaution of calling Islamabad Pakistan and had asked them if they meant for the elephant to be delivered to the zoo? He said the Pakistanis said, according to their instructions from their Mother, I mean Mullah, the elephant had to be delivered to the Zoo at 1121 Lincoln. The Postman told us also that the General Inspector had pointed out to the Pakistanis that the zoo was ..."

Sue's eyes started to quiver. My long story was getting the best of her. Her head bobbed. She caught herself falling asleep, and her eyes flashed open like a deer at night caught in the light of Wallstreem's parking lot. Deer often go to Wallstreem to nibble on lettuce heads and busted open packages of frozen peas. At night, their eyes sparkle in the shine of your transport's headlights. When Sue's eyes flashed open, I assaulted her with more of the elephant story and the mullahs of Pakistan. I even added a Russian subplot where Putin had gone back in time and placed a nuclear bomb aboard Sputnik and blasted everything to hell.

Finally, a plume of smoke shot straight up from the top of Sue's head. She leaned forward. A bit of drool from the casserole dribbled out of the side of her mouth. She was thoroughly discharged. This new government doesn't like to use the word dead. I peeped out the window. The soldiers seemed terribly confused. They had dressed or rather half dressed. Some wore pants but no shirts and vice versa. A few laughed and danced while others beat their chests and cried out.

Now what to do with Sue? I pondered over my options. She was a humanoid so she wouldn't stink up the place. If she had been recording our conversation, the government would wonder why her transmits ceased. Her Mercury transport with its silver fins was still parked in the driveway. I wondered if her stomach grinder was shot. I could disassemble her legs and set her up on the counter and use her for a food grinder. I heard peanut shells make an excellent mulch. Gods knows I got enough of them with that darn elephant in the backyard. Yep had to keep the elephant anyway even after Harold's lobotomy punishment. The government insisted they had not made any mistake in delivering the thing. Sometimes the elephant does give that postman a good dousing with water.

"Oh, Harold, what shall I do?" I wailed.

Harold just stared at the hole in Sue's head. I stared also. A nose-like something wiggled up through the hole. The nose was silver and pointed like a bullet.

"Oh my god!" I screamed out and jumped up to get my broom. When I came back, Sue's brain (neuron circuitry, NC for short) sat on table nibbling a bit of the casserole. When it saw me, it reared on its hind legs, hissed, and dashed off the table. I swiped at it with my broom, but it outran me. Its pointed nose aimed at the weakest part of the back door. I hit it and knocked it off course. The NC boomeranged off the stove, jumped two feet in the air and again headed for the door. I smashed it into the refrigerator unit. It lay still, stunned. I raised my broom high in the air and brought it down hard. My broom bounced upward, out of my hands and hit the ceiling light fixture. Sue's brain had activated a shield. Nothing could damage or stop it from its mission. It's that way with humanoids. When they discharge, the government tracking device calls their brains home to deprogram and use in another humanoid. It's sort of like reincarnation. Sue's brain shook itself, revved up on its hind legs. This time, its sharp nose bore a hole through my back door leaving a perfectly round opening the size of a tangerine.

I looked out the window. A swat member squatted and patted the NC. It squeaked furiously and pointed its nose toward my yard. Suddenly the soldiers picked up their guns and aimed their faces toward our domicile.

"Gosh, Harry, it's over for you and me. The Government will be coming for me in one of their long black vehicles. But Harry, your wife has made a stand in her own way. They will debrief Sue's brain. Those notes will be stashed in their sealed vaults. A thousand years from now when civilized men dig, they will find in a pile, a few dried bananas, human teeth, a Vanilla Ice CD, and a tattered paper entitled, "Notes on Mabel Singer." And those will be my words they read. People will learn of the government's atrocity against Mabel Singer and her husband, Harry. They'll say what horrible, horrible leaders those "Hoe and Moon" men were for ordinary people like us.

*iPodphonius—Another name for iPhone

####

About the Author

Charles W. Harvey is a native Houstonian and a graduate of the University of Houston. Charles was a 1st place prize recipient of PEN/ Discovery for Cheeseburger, which went on to be published in the Ontario Review. Harvey was also awarded the Cultural Arts Council of Houston Grant for Writers and Artists. Charles has been published in Soulfires, Story Magazine SHADE, High Infidelity, The James White Review, and recently NEWVERSENEWS. He is the author of the novels The Butterfly Killer, The Road to Astroworld, and Antoine's Double Trouble. He is also the author of several stories and poetry collections.

Connect with Harvey

Don't miss out!

Visit the website below and you can sign up to receive emails whenever Charles Harvey publishes a new book. There's no charge and no obligation.

https://books2read.com/r/B-A-EWG-PZEDB

BOOKS 2 READ

Connecting independent readers to independent writers.

Did you love *Rough Cut Until I Bleed*? Then you should read *3AM - Poems and Stories From the Other Mind*[1] by Charles Harvey!

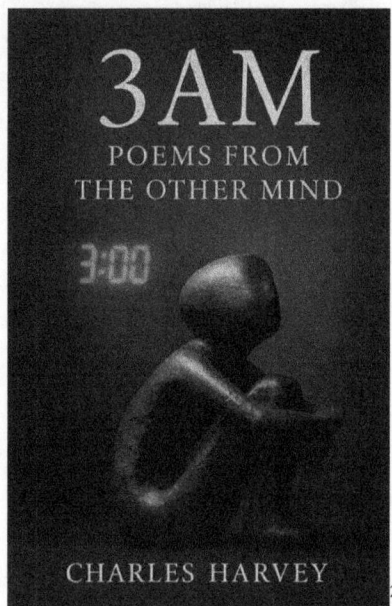

Read a poem a day!

Step into the enigmatic world of "3 AM Poems From the Other Mind," a poetry collection that defies the boundaries of comfort and dares to plunge you into the depths of thought and emotion. These poems, crafted in the hushed moments between midnight and dawn, are not for the faint of heart but for those seeking a poetic journey that will leave them breathless and transformed.

Like Allen Ginsberg's iconic "Howl," the verses within "3 AM" are unapologetically raw, provocative, and thought-provoking. They awaken the senses and ignite the mind, offering an experience that is both disquieting and electrifying. In the spirit of Robert Frost's

1. https://books2read.com/u/mvjga6

2. https://books2read.com/u/mvjga6

definition of poetry as the moment when emotion finds its thought and thought finds words, this collection delves deep into the well of human sentiment, unearthing profound and sometimes uncomfortable truths.

The witching hours are a time when the ordinary turns extraordinary, and these poems are no exception. They will transport you through the labyrinth of the subconscious, challenging your perspective and shaking you out of your comfort zone. Just as the cat on your lap may be startled by the sudden burst of energy in the room, you too will find yourself flying around the room of your own emotions, landing in a different perspective, forever changed.

"3 AM Poems From the Other Mind" is an invitation to embrace the mysterious, to wander through the uncharted territory of the human soul, and to confront the raw power of words that resonate with the darkest and most brilliant corners of the human experience. This collection is for those who seek not only comfort but also the exhilaration of poetic exploration that lingers long after the final page is turned.

Excerpts: **The Man in The Moon 1** Who's up at 2 am? The midnight oil has long burned out Sleep and sex roll restless On the worn mattress. Dreams escape the open eyes Shadows rattle the door Three o'clock is the witching hour Red ashes float from the patio Eyes across the courtyard catch you breathing. You look away only to look again. You know the lonely mattress would enjoy the company And your lilac-scented air could use some funk. But the night won't last a lifetime, so You slip back into your room and wonder, What if there is a man in the moon? **A Good Dog** The neighbor beats his dog at 3am and he don't stop I hear her tail beating the wall and he don't stop She gnaws on his bone and he don't stop All night long she whines and he don't stop Her collar and chain drags the floor and he don't stop She begs at the table and he don't stop She rolls over and plays dead and he don't stop She fetches his slippers and he don't stop She trees his birds and he don't stopShe has his puppiesand he don't stopAll in the wee hours I hearbitch bitch bitchand he don't stop.

Get 3AM Now!

Read more at https://charlesharveyauthor.wordpress.com.

Also by Charles Harvey

Astroworld
Short Stories From The Road to Astroworld
Promise's Letters From the Road to Astroworld

Buck Wile Stories
Buck Wile is Punk'd Out On Da Downlow
Buck Wile is Butt Naked In Da City

Catnip
Catnip Gray Cat Detective: The Tabitha Davenport Affair

Dogs Bark
When Dogs Bark the Short Story
Bark Too

Kiss
The Beginning of John Henry and Alphonse

Poetic Journeys
Americana
3AM - Poems and Stories From the Other Mind
The Last Supper
Rough Cut Until I Bleed

Roommates
Roommates and The Old Dead Seaman
Roommates and Other Stories

Standalone
Coming Home Tomorrow
Cheeseburger
My Manhood is Very Important to Me
Betty's House
Black Queen
How I Got Over
Insects and Elephants
Minister Q
Othello Jones
The Blue Train To Heaven
The Power Plant
Ebenezer Jenkins' Christmas in Chicago
Q is a Bad Letter and Other QQ Crazy Stories
Antoine's Double Trouble
Maura And Her Two Husbands
The 520i
No Satisfaction

Urban Tales
Into the Murky Water
Red Underwear
Cheeseburger and Other Stories
Kirby Bob Understands Heaven
A Foursome Plus Poems
Cruising in the Name of Love

Watch for more at https://charlesharveyauthor.wordpress.com.

About the Author

Charles W. Harvey is a native Houstonian and a graduate of the University of Houston. At UofH he studied fiction under the guidance of Rosellen Brown and Chitra Divakaruni. In 1987, Charles was a 1st place prize recipient of PEN/Discovery for his short story Cheeseburger, which went on to be published in the Ontario Review. In 1989 Charles Harvey was awarded the Cultural Arts Council of Houston Grant for Writers and Artists. Also in 1989 he was a finalist in the MacDonald's Literary Achievement Awards. Charles has been published in Soulfires, Story Magazine SHADE, High Infidelity, The James White Review, and others. He is the author of the novels The Butterfly Killer, The Road to Astroworld, and Antoine's Double Trouble. He is also the author of several story and poetry collections. He also writes for the stage and screen.

Read more at https://charlesharveyauthor.wordpress.com.

About the Publisher

Wes Writers and Publishers strives to bring you great books for your reading pleasure. We have been in the business of producing quality works of fiction for over two decades. We will branch out in the future to add more authors to bring you the reader, very high quality and entertaining stories from all genres. It begins with Charles W. Harvey our star prize winning literary writer an poet. He is the author of the prize winning short story Cheeseburger selected by Joyce Carol Oates in the 1987 PEN/Southwest Prize. He is a frequent participant in NANOWRIMO and other literary endeavors. Please feel free to sample his many stories and two Novels via Smashwords and other fine retailers. AC Adams brings you a little something different. He is our premier author for the gay literary erotica genre. Many of our readers have enjoyed his Roommates series. Look forward for a lot more to come from this up and coming author. Clarissa Haley comes from east Texas. She likes quirky little stories that swim around that brain of hers. She has several exciting projects in the works. She has a few romance stories in the works for future release Wes Writers and Publishers (we like being called WWP) will be adding more l writers under its wings in the near future. We love good stories.

Read more at https://charlesharveyauthor.wordpress.com.

www.ingramcontent.com/pod-product-compliance
Lightning Source LLC
Chambersburg PA
CBHW032006040426
42448CB00006B/504